What's Up in Architecture

W. G. ROGERS

HARCOURT, BRACE & WORLD, INC. | NEW YORK

What's Up in Architecture

A LOOK AT MODERN BUILDING

Illustrated with photographs

For my wife, Mildred Weston,
with thanks as always for her help

The author and the publisher acknowledge with thanks
the permission of the publishers, Horizon Press,
to reprint passages from *The Future of Architecture*
by Frank Lloyd Wright. Copyright 1953.

Contents

What's Up in Architecture

"There is not a man on earth who cannot be helped in some way by an architect."

—*Claude-Nicolas Ledoux, Architect to the King of France*

1 | The New Look

Our world has taken on an exciting new look. It crept in around us imperceptibly. Perhaps the first hint of it was a curious house on the edge of town, boxlike, with a flat roof. Or it was a grain elevator, a warehouse, or an airplane hangar. People mistrusted this look even more than they mistrusted the first autos and planes. Autos and planes were brand-new contraptions so that differences were to be expected. For a house, there was a tried and trusted age-old model. Why not stick to it? To most people, as to their fathers, a bank building was a row of pillars, a department store was like a French château, a railroad station was patterned on Roman baths, and a town hall was a temple with a dome borrowed from antiquity.

But a bank is not pillars. It is vaults, moneybags, and wicket windows. A department store is display areas, counters, and convenient aisles. Pillars, needed to hold up a roof two thousand years ago, can be dispensed with. Some modern roofs hold themselves up without much of anything to support them. We might think they floated. Bricks can be almost as flimsy as a curtain and still do the job required. We call the wall most commonly in use today a curtain wall. Propriety and fitness should be the guides just as they were in the golden ages. The old cathedrals were stone, and they looked it magnificently, every inch. The new cathedrals, to be as true in spirit to their own age, deserve to have the look of steel and concrete. There is nothing specially holy about stone, or nothing that is not just as holy about steel and concrete.

The architect has covered more ground with his advanced ideas than we realize. We owe new sounds to the composer and novel appearances to the painter—who, as we shall see, has been allied on occasion with the architect. In theory, most modern music could have been written long ago and all modern painting painted in some previous period. But modern architecture, which began about the same time as the new painting and music, was never possible before. Like atomic fission or space flight, it belongs inescapably and exclusively in the twentieth century. Even if people had thought of it, they lacked the wherewithal to create it. It would be as hard to make a skyscraper out of wood two-by-fours and shingles as a silk purse out of a sow's ear. Hammer and nails, saw and bit and ruler did the jobs peculiar to the past. To build a bridge or a dome today, computers are needed. Even the arithmetic employed by the new men would be incomprehensible to their predecessors.

Near miracles can be performed with reinforced concrete.

Steel is stronger than anything used in a pyramid, a Parthenon, a Pantheon. Perhaps even the ancient glories can be surpassed by the modern architect when he has time to acquaint himself with the potentialities of modern means. He has already worked wonders.

He has faced the same uphill struggle as the painter. The public stubbornly wanted what it was used to. It stayed faithful to the old familiar tunes and to the old familiar pictures on the walls and to the old familiar walls as well. Custom, habit, tradition, prejudice, and a streak of ordinary laziness thwarted the modernist. He had to fight every step of the way. This was an art, but it had nothing cloistered about it. It was also a great and thunderous battle. It directly involves you and me. It touches us at as many places and as frequently as the deeds of our generals and presidents, our preachers and teachers.

2 | A Walk

We listen to music from a seat in a concert hall or beside our radio, TV set, or record player. We read a book relaxed in a soft chair at home. To look at paintings, we do nothing more strenuous than stroll through a museum.

But architecture is not for the lazy man. It obliges him to get up and walk about. To be sure, there is architecture inside the house, but there is more outside, all up and down every street. It stretches from the center of the town or city out into the country. We need tickets for the theater and a card to borrow books from the library. But architecture itself is as free as a tree or a hill or a view, and it is practically everywhere. The theater and library with or without ticket and card are architecture. So are our homes, the yards surrounding them, our schools, the walks, roads, and streets to and from them, the office, factory, bank, and church. The architect lays out the grounds around the buildings and puts up the stands in the baseball park, the garages, gas stations, and bus terminals. It is hard to find a pie he does not have a finger in.

Lots of us take walks. Do we look around? Do we bother to decide: here is an ugly spot, there is a sight we love? Do we ask ourselves why? Let's try a walk, or rather two walks and two looks with them. They can be as exciting as a game. We start and finish the first without stirring from our chairs. For the second we get up and move about. Even so, the first may be harder because it occurs in the imagination only. Yesterday is easy to remember and so is last Christmas. But let's think still farther back and picture our home and town as they were seventy-five or a hundred years ago. Perhaps we see them most clearly by shutting our eyes.

To get to a place of business or to school in those days, a man and woman, a boy and girl started out about as they do now. Their clothes might look different to us but nowhere near so different as other things. People lived in a two-story house or an apartment building occupied by only six or eight families. The young folks skipped down the stairs, the elders went at a slower pace. Their ways led along brick walks. Houses sat well back. Wide lawns were dotted with shrubs, flowers, or trees. Trees also grew between walk and curb in a narrow stretch of grass.

Boys and girls in the country attended the little red schoolhouse. It had one teacher, one room, one stove, one row of hooks for hats and coats, one blackboard, one door, and one single window or at the most pair of windows per side to admit some squares of light. City children had their red schoolhouse, too, made of brick, two or maybe three stories high. Holes were cut at regular intervals for windows. With too many holes and too many missing bricks, it might fall down, even though the wall was at least a foot thick. Now we might think it was more like a fort than a school. Even the few windows that were provided required heavy stone lids across the top to support the burden under which glass and fragile frame would crack and crumble. Sometimes the oblong slabs, gray, white, or yellow, were carved with a flower, vine, or scroll. Though some desks were dark in full sunlight, there were roll-down curtains when needed. Baseball was played around in back on a sand lot.

The businessman walked to his office in ten or fifteen minutes, unless he drove his horse and buggy or rode in a horsecar. A laborer spent his days in a dingy, sooty factory built smack up against the sidewalk. A passer-by peered through the windows at the machines, the spinning belts and wheels, the puffs of steam. The thump, roar, and hiss of the shop could be heard a mile away. The tall chimney belched such black smoke that the housewife must constantly be sweeping, mopping, and dusting. But a lot of her trouble was homemade. She burned coal in her stoves in the kitchen and living room and the newfangled central furnace, which blew stinging hot air through floor vents. The coal stood beside the upstairs stoves in hods brought up from the bin in the cellar. There was coal dust. To shake the grate, sift the ashes, and pick out the clinkers spread a grayish film all over the furniture. Home was not much cleaner than the factory, the factory not much dirtier than home. Every place contributed to the supply of grime.

The bank stood grandly on the Courthouse Square, which was crisscrossed by walks and prettied up with plots of green. Around the green were the grocery, the hardware store, the courthouse itself, the church, and the general store.

The grocery had a display window and a canvas awning. The courthouse was gray stone, yellow brick, or both, and it looked as stout as a castle. Strings of little windows with small panes never let in enough light. They were supposed to be for looks, or somebody's idea of looks. A porch extended across the front of the bank. Tall, white, and fluted round pillars held up the forward edge of the roof, or pretended to. We have seen pictures of just such roofs with pillars in books telling about two-thousand-year-old Athens and Rome. The church might be the kind often found in New England: wood painted white with steeple and belfry and an open railed balcony. The entrance was at the top of a long flight of steps. Grandmother wished they were not so many and not so steep, but she admitted they did help the church to rise up high and dignified, the way it should. The peaked windows and the steps remind us of other pictures from our histories.

After school a boy went to the swimming hole or walked out in the country. The country was easy to find since it began right where the town left off. The dividing line was sharp and clear: end of the sidewalk, end of the pavement, end of the street lights, and the last house.

The boy's father was a kibitzer; he liked to see how Mr. Smith was getting along with the building of his house. The lumberyard team had delivered piles of boards and two-by-fours. A couple of sawhorses were set up; a ladder lay on the ground. The cellar hole was dug, a stone wall solidly cemented inside it, and the foundation timbers lay level in place. Mr. Smith had raised his framing for the first floor. His helper the carpenter wore a stiff apron. He had a pocketful of nails. A big, round-handled, low, flat tray contained more nails, saws, a ruler that flipped open to six feet, screws, screwdriver, hammer, bit, plane, a level, a file, a dull-colored and leadlike right angle. At the moment, he was finishing a window opening. He took a measurement, chose a clean board with no knotholes to mar it, guided his flat-sided thick pencil along the right angle to mark it, steadied the board on the sawhorses with hand and knee, and went to work with his crosscut saw. Every single separate piece of wood to be fitted into the frame had to be measured, sawed, perhaps planed down, and nailed or screwed in place. The boy's father admired the careful workman. The way to build a house to last, he believed, was to have good seasoned timber and a good seasoned carpenter.

For a brick house Mr. Smith hired a bricklayer. On the ground were a pile of bricks, bags of cement, a cone of sand. Boards were nailed together to form a miniature pool or basin. Into it were dumped sand and cement sluiced down with water. With the aid of a hoe, it was mixed to mortar of the perfect consistency to slap and pat around with a diamond-shaped trowel. The bricklayer began at ground level and worked up. How else could he set one brick on top of another?

Mr. Smith's street was macadam, cobblestone, or hard-packed dirt. It was lighted by gas or oil like the lamps at home.

The town had a livery stable, a railroad station with flower boxes, a hotel with a wide front porch, and a grain and feed store. The houses, shingled and clapboarded, were often decorated with bay windows. Gables broke the plain, even pitch of the roofs. The posts of piazzas and balconies had filigreed tops. The balusters of the railings bulged, thinned, and rounded to suit the whim of the man who turned them on the lathe. Many communities boasted an opera house. But its doors swung open less for opera than for graduation exercises, church services, and social gatherings. The family always hoped Father would not get seats right behind the thick pillars that supported the balcony.

All this *used* to be. Those of us who listened long ago to our grandparents have found this imaginary walk easy. What we have visited was the setting of their childhood. We examined it in the mind's eye. Today it does not exist anywhere else. Drastic and fundamental changes in our environment have occurred in three generations. We talk the same language as the old people and read many of the same books. Their pictures, music, and clothes are largely familiar. But the background, the visual and physical aspect of their lives, differs astoundingly from ours. The curtain has risen on brand-new scenery. If we just lift our eyes from this page, they fall on very minor examples of the very great revolutionary advances. The electric light replaces oil and gas, the electric refrigerator replaces the icebox, the radiator replaces the stove. Sealed windows and air conditioning keep out dust. Such changes, spread out and vastly amplified, affect our entire lives. They are at bottom architectural.

3 | Another Walk

Now we start the second, the real walk. For anyone not used to hoofing it, a car waits in the carport about where the woodshed or carriage house once stood but squeezed in a lot closer. Or there is transportation by bicycle, bus, and subway. "Livery Stable," the painted wood sign, has disappeared. Rows of electric lights flash, pennants flutter, a figure spins on a pedestal, balls whirl, or something does something else to draw attention to the gas station or parking lot. The plain barn with one huge door has yielded to broad spreads of glass and roofs angled every which way. Tiles replace weathered boards. Pungent automobile exhaust has blown away the smells of the stable.

A boy or girl or a teacher from a century back would never guess the little red schoolhouse had blossomed out into this new meandering shape. Whether in the middle of a city or out in the country, it has no thick brick walls, deep-set windows, or extra top story. Once school meant a walk, perhaps a long one. Now the teacher drives and pupils arrive in buses. Built low, often with concrete blocks, it sprawls over a lot of ground. If there is still only one window per room or one pair, it is big enough to fill an entire side. Nobody sits where it is too dark or has trouble reading the blackboard. The problem may be too much light. Instead of roll curtains there are blinds of adjustable narrow slats. In the southland there may be colored glass panels to tone down the glare, or sun breakers have been constructed. Developed by a French architect, they are like eyelids to the eye: wide projecting slabs of the building itself keep desks shaded and cool.

The team does not play on any sand lot out back but a mile away on a spanking new athletic field with immense grandstand and soaring bleachers. The school has a machine shop, laboratory, sewing machines, and gas or electric stoves. Long fluorescent tubes provide lighting—no more oil lamps in classrooms, in the streets, or at home, no more matches to keep safe in a tight tin box. Push or turn a button for heat as well as light. For stove, coal hod, and bin, there is substituted an oil tank or simply gas pipes or wiring.

The railroad station may have turned into a bus station. The biggest thing around is the airport terminal. A boy starting for school or a man for work does not go down the stairs; he rides in the elevator. Sidewalks are concrete not brick. No room is left for neat grassy oblongs. Trees have been cut down to satisfy our greediest and most demanding invention: the auto. Anyone who wants to stretch his legs in the country actually has a hard time finding it. It has been

beaten back farther and farther. In every direction outside
every city, thousands of acres are dotted with housing devel-
opments. One house is the copy of the next house, one development the copy of the next development, one mile outside
my city the copy of one mile outside yours. They threaten to
gobble up all the land. The best we can do for woods and
fields is spend all morning driving to them and all afternoon
driving back.

The bank has lost its pillars. It is only one story high. The
walls are pared down to panes of plate glass, which the blow
of a hammer could crack. Larger expanses of desks and
counters are more simply and openly arranged. The pitched
roof has been pressed down flat. The courthouse is not a
hodgepodge of brick, stone, and trim. It has lost its look of a
castle. The theater has chopped away the pillars that blocked
sight lines. The church has no steps and perhaps no steeple
and belfry, either. The windows are not like anything in picture books about ancient cathedrals. But grandmother still
complains, not because she loses her breath but because this
barer edifice is not what she is used to. She is afraid it is not
intimate enough. She wonders whether it is as comforting a
place for prayer.

What does Mr. Smith do now about a house? He buys
fewer clapboards and shingles, and they are metal or composition instead of wood. Walls are of different materials, texture, and color.

Perhaps the strangest sight is the bricklayer. He now can
begin in mid-air, at the fifth floor or the tenth. It must be
magic. How can one brick be laid without another under it?
They used to hold up floors and roof; now it must be they
hang from the top as well as support it. Some old function
has been denied them. They still keep out wind, cold, and

rain, but they perform as bricks have not done since the days of the Persians, Egyptians, and Romans centuries ago. The brick wall is not a brick wall any longer.

The bricklayer may have another surprise for us. Instead of mortaring one brick at a time, he handles a solid panel of fifty, a hundred, or more. They come now in the economy size: the biggest lots ever. No hod carrier has to sweat up the ladder to the scaffolding with them. The swift cable of a derrick hoists them. Sawhorses, piles of boards, and carpenter's tools are not so necessary. Neither is the carpenter himself or, for that matter, the bricklayer. A lot of their work is done behind the scenes in the factory. A building is not made out of bricks but panels of them, not out of single boards but many of them fixed in a frame, not out of bits of a window but entire windows. They are made to fit before reaching the holes they fit into. A wall may be prebuilt in two-story sections that need only to be bolted in place. An entire skyscraper can be walled in in one week. The builder has turned into the assembler. He seems to play with blocks. They come ready-made; he shuffles them together.

The supermarket replaces the store. Apartment houses hold twenty, thirty, fifty families. The factory, all glass surface, clean and shiny, may have moved like the school into the middle of nowhere. Out in the country, if the chimney belches smoke, no homes catch the soot. Instead of walking to work, men drive or ride bus or train, or both, or all three. But what took ten minutes formerly may run to five or ten times as long in our crowded world. The rush hour is when it does no good to rush.

These things all so different, so excitingly replacing the old, the things we live in, walk by, and use along our streets, in our squares, homes, offices, schools, and factories, and

also some of the things not so good, the hindrances, the dis-
advantages, and the interferences—all these things are what
this book is about: architecture.

There is specialization among architects. Some plan the
throughways that span our map like ribbons—or, as has been
charged, like chains. Some plant our grounds. Some put up
buildings. One specializes in schools, another in factories,
another in bridges, and another in monster agglomerations
like Rockefeller Center, which originally covered some ten
acres and is spreading out cancerously. Some specialize in
parks, some in over-all town planning. Is the kitchen stove
placed handily with relation to sink and pantry? Is the light
switch good? Can it be reached easily? Does some projecting
corner of a chair, table, or bed reach out and leave us with a
black-and-blue spot? It all adds up to architecture. Look
down on the earth from a plane and the general aspect is
architectural. Look up from your chair and what you see is
architectural.

4 | Materials

However impatient we are for the future to move in on us, the past gets in its way. This heritage lies all around. We notice a railroad station dated 1900 or 1910. We live in a weathered house or apartment. Once in a while we still see a barn—do not underrate barns. The French poet and drama-tist Paul Claudel said his travels all over the world never showed him a more beautiful building than the simple stone barn at the twelfth-century Abbaye d'Hautecombe beside the Lac du Bourget.

Many still serviceable survivors and the settled streets they occupy remind us of our first imaginary walk. Or they can be several hundred years old. Wood, stone, brick, and rough concrete have been till now the universal materials. As long as they were in use, the aspect of an environment changed only slightly. A sixteenth-century man might have felt at home in an eighteenth-century street almost anywhere in Europe.

But in our day some potent magic has gotten loose. The architect has waved his wand. A man from any era prior to the last hundred years would be dumfounded and incredulous before many sights that are commonplace to us.

One reason for the extraordinary changes is of course the demand for kinds of shelters not dreamed of before. There have always been theaters, churches, palaces, halls. Now there are motels, garages, reactor plants, disposal plants, hangars, warehouses, bus stations, airports—ancient Greece and Rome supply no models for them. The unique purposes, novel materials, and our vastly intensified know-how are responsible for the unique twentieth-century look. We cannot help ourselves.

It is a peculiarly, characteristically American look. We cannot claim the most distinguished writers, composers, or dancers for our country. If we have pioneered in painting, we have done so only recently. But for a good three-quarters of a century, more often than any other people, we have been the architectural leaders of the West. What has been done *to* us has been done *by* us. The architectural story is our story. That makes it all the more exciting.

The Greeks piled up monster blocks of stone, square and round, plain and fluted. The Romans did circuses, temples, and markets usually with brick and mortar. Antiquity's most famous dome crowning the Pantheon by the Tiber River is ordinary large flat bricks plus coarse mortar. About a hundred and forty feet high, it is the same in diameter. Its rim rests on walls twenty feet thick. If they were thinner, the enormous weight on top would have crushed them or pried them apart. The Romanesque church and Gothic cathedral were stone. England and America depended more commonly on wood, cheap, plentiful, and easily worked. It was used for houses and sometimes for even the biggest churches. Thanks to an ingenious system of triangle shapes or trusses, it could lift a heavy timber and slate roof to a peak high in the air. The construction resembled that of a ship turned upside down. The intricate frame for one served as well in reverse for the other.

With what do we build now? Iron, steel and many alloys, glass in the largest sheets ever rolled, plastics unknown to our predecessors, imitation stone and brick, tiles, aluminum, wallboard, plywood. The most versatile and challenging medium is concrete. Developed and improved as never before, plain, reinforced, precast, prestressed, it consists of an aggregate of sand and stone and portland cement. This is a hydraulic cement, that is, it hardens when mixed with water. It has been available for a hundred and fifty years, but only now are its full potentialities being appreciated.

To fashion a clay figure, we knead it with our fingers. So that the soft stuff will cling together better, it is sometimes applied around a wood skeleton. The sculptor calls this core or dummy an armature; he pats the clay onto it firmly. To make a concrete wall or pillar, we first construct a container, a form, a mold, usually boards nailed together for this purpose alone. The wet concrete, which flows like cake batter, is then poured in. We have seen eight- and ten-wheeled trucks rumbling through the streets bearing a huge slowly revolving cylinder. It is filled with transit-mixed concrete. It starts the trip as cement and aggregate and ends at the construction site as concrete of the right consistency. Like the jello in the fancy dessert form, it stands till it hardens. Then the boards are knocked away. The resulting surface may be left raw or polished, and the job is done. Or concrete may be reinforced; that is, it has its own armature. Steel rods are run through the middle of the space fashioned for the mix. An old wall in the course of demolition shows the steel sticking out like spikes where the blows of the sledge have crumbled the casing. Or as a wall is built, rods fixed in a finished slab protrude to anchor and strengthen the slab that will congeal at the next pouring.

Reinforced concrete was patented by an American, Thaddeus Hyatt, in 1878. The first reinforced-concrete framed building came from the drawing board of François Hennebique in France. The brothers Auguste and Gustave Perret, who studied at the Ecole des Beaux-Arts in Paris, opened an office early in this century. In their initial efforts, they handled concrete like wood or stone, just as the first auto was made to resemble a buggy minus the shafts. They molded beams and blocks and topped a doorway with a concrete beam in the classical post-and-lintel fashion. But as ancient builders thought in stone and wood, the Perrets learned to think in concrete. Not the Beaux-Arts faculty but concrete itself was their true teacher. From it they found out how to work it.

Early timid advances with the new materials were not propitious. The man with some untried means at his disposal was never quite sure what he could do with it. Cast iron had been produced in England by 1735. For decades no one dreamed of substituting this dull, cold, coarse bar for wood or stone with their handsome colors, grain, and texture. England had a cast-iron bridge before the end of the century. In 1801, a more ambitious one was proposed, though not erected, with a six-hundred-foot span to cross the Thames at London.

In New York City in 1848, James Bogardus built a five-story structure that must have struck some people as a freak. All the weight rested, not on the immemorial wood, stone or composite piers, or on the walls, but on cast iron. Bogardus had the honesty, unless it was naïveté, not to hide it. It showed frankly as support and was left uncovered plainly in the façade. This cast iron was not ashamed of itself. Still more of it was exposed significantly in the 1880's in Chicago by a second bold builder, Major William Le Baron Jenney, in his Home Insurance Building. Jenney was too arty and masked it with masonry, but it actually supported both the floors and the walls. Halfway to the top of the ten-story structure he was putting up, he was informed by a Carnegie company in Pittsburgh that Bessemer steel was available and better suited to his job. It replaced iron in the upper stories. Crude and homely to the eye, this was technically a sky-scraper.

Sometimes a man had his doubts. Could an iron bar be as strong as a stone three times its size? The manufacturer said so. Maybe this was just his sales pitch. The cautious architect hid it under concrete or laid a sheet of stone across it or disguised it with a coat of paint. Yet steel actually lived up to specifications, he soon learned. It had three times the strength of granite, which had three times the strength of sandstone. It was thirty times as strong as limestone.

In 1885, Burnham & Root adopted Jenney's skeleton for Chicago's twelve-story Rookery Building. Compared to many other cities, Chicago has a disability: it rests on a soil that gives. The problem of building on ground that, in effect, would like to get out from under is not new. The Leaning Tower of Pisa is on unfirm ground. A spectacular example is Mexico, D.F. Once the site of a great body of water, it is now covered with a few soaring skyscrapers and many constructions of tremendous weight. The ancient lake bed tends to slide out from under them. The massive cathedral on the principal square, the Zócalo, has sunk a foot or so. Or to put it another way, to the eye the sidewalk appears to have pushed up higher on the walls. A few miles north, the Shrine of Our Lady of Guadalupe presents an astonishing sight. The basilica seems firmly and evenly settled. The vast structure right beside it has tipped; it is Mexico's Leaning Tower, but infinitely bulkier than the one in Pisa. In Chicago, the ground is so dependably unstable that sidewalks beside new buildings used to be slanted up from the curb in the certainty they would sink and in the hope they would sink, all together, somewhere near the definitive level. To meet this problem, Burnham & Root, thanks to modern materials, hit on a different type of foundation. Their predecessors constructed huge pyramid-like forms of concrete and rock that had to be sunk to a costly depth. The new men balanced their Rookery on crosspieces of steel rails set in concrete. Three feet down was deep enough. They acted more like pads than posts.

Builders kept learning and experimenting and playing with new ideas. In 1887, William Holabird and Martin Roche, who owed their professional start to Jenney, put up the fourteen-story Tacoma Building in Chicago. Built on a corner, it had two fronts and two rears. The walls out of sight were of traditional construction to hold up floors and roof. The others were modern style. The principal burden rested on cast-iron columns with steel beams spanning the space between. The brick and terra-cotta surfaces had it easy; they did not support anything except brick and terra cotta. They had no chore beyond looking attractive and keeping out the weather. Here for the first time the bricklayer began his work in mid-air, or at any convenient floor level.

Though Europe and England ventured in the same avant-garde direction, there was little communication of ideas. We were as ignorant of their progress as they of ours. At the start of the nineteenth century, an English factory needed open, unencumbered space for big machines. But no one knew how to hold up the ceiling with columns set more than ten and fifteen feet apart. Only half a century later another factory could space them fifty feet apart. Structural iron had proved its worth. By 1871, France claimed the first factory with an all-iron frame; it made Menier chocolate. But iron was still a material for which the gentleman builder foolishly blushed. John Nash used a lot of it in a pavilion in the resort town of Brighton, England. But he hated to admit it, so he painted it to imitate the stuff popular with contemporary decorators, a stuff, oddly, with practically no strength at all: bamboo.

5 | Architect-Engineer

Besides new needs and kinds of buildings and materials, the demand for more buildings of all types, old as well as new, grew rapidly. There just were not enough roofs.

Cities have always been with us, but until today they have been manageable. We could live in them and like it; we had enough neighbors, but they left us elbow room. Paris, London, and New York counted perhaps several hundred thousand people, no more.

Suddenly and uncomfortably we felt a squeeze. While our world seemed to shrink, the numbers that must fit into available space multiplied. It is called the population explosion. There also came a rush from the farms. Urban centers swelled monstrously, New York and Tokyo climbing toward ten million. Where ten enterprises occupied a street before, a hundred now fight for a window and a door that look on it. The only way to provide this room was to build higher. People and offices stopped being side by side and began to be over and under. That increased the value of the land ten times.

It was idle to disapprove of this change. The forces behind it seemed irresistible. One tall building begat another. Ten and twelve stories climbed up to sixteen and twenty. Such heights did not faze the eager architects. They made their first efforts in Chicago, once the unrivaled architectural center of this country. The first true skyscraper, skyscraper in its build from top to bottom and in its looks, owes a lot to Chicago. If we had a guess, we would probably say it was erected in New York. We would be wrong. The place was St. Louis, Missouri. It was the Wainwright Building, and it still stands there.

The know-how for building up and up toward unprecedented heights would have counted for nothing without the elevator, first used in New York in 1853. Edinburgh, Scotland, already had ten-story tenements, but the walk-up wore out all but the hardiest occupants.

The new world was the handiwork of the new men. Perhaps the times drove them to their surprising deeds, but they were the ones responsible. They did not invent. One architect declares correctly that no style was ever invented. It was born out of contemporary opportunities, invitations, and challenges. These men condemned new building that did not employ new materials. They spurned the methods inherited from a long-dead century. They demanded a clean slate— and even slate was no longer good enough. A pillar had no decorative value when it had no practical value. The only way the Greeks could keep the roof off their necks was to shore it up with pillars. Out of this necessity, they created masterpieces like the Parthenon and the beautiful temple to Poseidon at Cape Sounion. Today the architect declares that handsome is as handsome does. Thus he determinedly abandons columns and cornices. His basic question was: What was wrong with replacing stone with steel? He answered confidently: Nothing. His trouble was that so many people preferred good old stone. The architect felt no sentimental attachment to stone. He loved its texture, its grain, its heft, and its appearance of indestructibility. But this love must not interfere with his deeper love for economic, efficient, and modern means.

Houses cannot be isolated any more. Neighbors are bound to worry over a new building. It means more noise, unpleasant odors, overcrowding, more traffic hazards. Thus architecture has branched out protectively beyond the house to include the street, the neighborhood, the entire town or city, the approaches to it. The architect is more than one man; he is a whole office; he is a bundle of know-hows. Sometimes his capacity goes under the title of engineering.

The inhabitant of a city enjoys membership in the community of his fellows. But he is increasingly aware that this wild urban growth may overpower and crush him. He has tried to rein it in, but his efforts, though they were ingenious and varied, were usually ineffective.

Heavy population concentrations in nineteenth-century England resulted from the rush for jobs in the mills. Rapid changes forced poor families into filthy tenements. Mill owners often ignored their wretchedness. But there was an Englishman who attacked what we sometimes fear is the insoluble problem of the metropolis. His name was Ebenezer

Howard. His particular target was the company town. We had them, too, centered on a mill in New England or a mine in Pennsylvania. Howard blamed the city for its brutal exclusion of the country. Acres of green, he said, should counteract the spread of asphalt. If state ownership of the land was too radical for him, some local control was necessary, he was sure, for the good of all. His ideal community was christened Garden City. People numbering thirty thousand would both live and work there. On his map the railroad station stood at the perimeter. Woods separated factories from homes; thus, living quarters would be free of industrial grime.

Not until the 1880's did we, in the United States, or one or two of us, envisage the purely modern problem of wheeled fast traffic, carriages first and then cars. The pioneer, still another type of architect, was Frederick Law Olmsted. Beginning in 1857, he was superintendent of New York City's Central Park. The contemporary French architect Le Corbusier has praised New Yorkers for preventing any encroachment on this eight-hundred-acre tract. The praise must be qualified. Greedy promoters had to be fought off year after year. Only recently they schemed crudely to pare down one edge for parking space and another edge for a restaurant. The place is all the more precious because it is about the only green New Yorkers can enjoy. Olmsted was so harried by politicians itching for his priceless acres that he resigned his post several times, but he won his battle.

His victory over trespassers was only one achievement. His ideal development of his entire acreage has guided the wise planning of parks and thoroughfares ever since. There are, he observed, different kinds of traffic. One must not interfere with another. He laid out separate ways for the man on horseback, the man on a bicycle, the man on foot, and the man on business hurrying to cross the park—today the autoist. If traffic does not move pretty much according to these principles, it comes near not moving at all.

The layman's record in planning and building is not all bad. He was there long before the expert. He plotted his streets as best he could, straight if possible, avoiding hills. Or he hammered together his own doghouse or woodshed. Or like Mr. Smith, he had the ambition to put up his home. The general assumption has been that a man had the wit to build whatever he needed. A training in the arts might help, but where in the past could he study architecture? Michelangelo, the sculptor, was ordered to mount the giant dome on the basilica of St. Peter's. The Popes summoned Bramante and Raphael from their easels to labor on papal halls and walls. John Vanbrugh, artist and playwright, built the vast palace of Blenheim, where Winston Churchill was born. Christopher Wren, specialist in anatomy and astronomy, was diverted to architecture to help reconstruct London after the Great Fire of 1666—and that was not the only conflagration to launch an architectural career. Inigo Jones also began as an artist. The strangest switch was managed by a gardener, Joseph Paxton. He, in effect, piled greenhouse on greenhouse to get the enormous Crystal Palace built in 1851 in London as an exhibition hall.

It is hard and sometimes impossible to draw the line between architect and engineer. The engineer knocked the posts out from under the theater balcony and began the bricklayer's work ten stories up. The architect knows what he wants done; the engineer tells him how to do it. The architect may be described as the idea man. Inspired by a dream—though engineers, too, have dreams—he longs for a world more beautiful and more characteristic of this century than of any past age. He wants it to match our automobile as our grandfather's world matched the horse and buggy—but the engineer deserves credit for the measuring mark itself: the auto and the roads it runs on. It is essential not to overestimate either one. They both helped thin down the old wall and replace it with wide glass windows. The engineer made trains and planes and machines for the manufacturer, and usually the architect housed them. Customarily a combination gets the job done. They may be different men or one man endowed with the two capacities. Together, they erect the skyscraper, the bridge that always before defied us, and the roof that curves almost miraculously high above spectators at the athletic field, the race track, or the bowling alley.

The Italian who has put up some of the most daring, thin-shelled, far-spreading roofs in the world, now or ever, is Pietro Luigi Nervi. He is the key creative figure in the superb bus terminal at the New York City end of the George Washington Bridge—itself a triumph of architectural-engineering vision. A plaque acknowledging Nervi's role lists him not as an architect but rather, as he styles himself, an engineer. Yale University in New Haven, Connecticut, has an Ingalls Hockey Rink. It amounts chiefly to an envelope draped from a vast curving concrete spine. This is by the Finnish-born American, Eero Saarinen, classified as an architect. We shall return to him and Nervi later. John Augustus and Washington Augustus Roebling, father and son, built the historic Brooklyn Bridge. They were not exactly engineers, not exactly architects. Their profession was wire rope making.

Some names connected with the monuments of antiquity are lost. Ictinus and Callicrates, architects both, were responsible for the Parthenon. We know in what dynasties the pyramids were erected in Egypt and who raised some arches and columns in the Roman Forum. But who is the man to whom we are everlastingly indebted for the Pont du Gard in southern France? Superb engineering teamed with superb architecture on this aqueduct built nearly two thousand years ago.

We shall say more about architects than engineers. More of the men in these pages—and the occasional women—are identified as architects. But a streak of the engineer runs through them all, as all engineers named here have a wide architectural vein. There is genius in both.

It used to be enough to know that a stone fresh from its quarry bed was easier to saw than after exposure to the air. It was enough to know that stone, like wood, has a grain and is strongest in one direction. A bricklayer built all the wall a man wanted. The carpenter's hammer and saw accomplished all that was expected of him. Who would need to ask an architect or engineer how to lay bricks or nail two-by-fours together? Once upon a time the real house was not much more intricate than one made out of children's blocks.

Now major construction is complex beyond imagining. Brains play a much bigger part than brawn. Muscle counts for nothing in the era of derrick, bulldozer, and other power machines. An architect's office may be as elaborate as a factory. Or he may fill as much space with his plans as the building he plans will actually occupy. Instead of being the jack of all trades, he is the master of all. He acts as the absolute ruler. His word must be law. The house we live in, the safety of the bridge over which thousands pass in all weather, the fifty-million-dollar investment in a skyscraper are his absolute responsibility. Who has more power? Who needs it more?

6 | Early Successes

Only an uncommon alertness can pinpoint the changes taking place immediately around us. Few people saw any future for the horseless carriage, which either chugged along deafeningly or stalled and was hauled away by the farmer's team. Few saw any future in the contraption the Wright brothers managed to lift into the air at Kitty Hawk. Few saw any significance in the first mass-produced nail, the first oil well, the first Bessemer steel.

The isolated, haphazard advances of modern architecture did not impress anybody very much, either. A look around showed—people thought—nothing compared to the monuments of the past. Perhaps it did not occur to them that the new tower or bridge was more than tower or bridge, more than a spectacle at a fair or a way to cross a river. Retrospect helps us to appreciate their prophetic character.

Anyone hunting for signs of the morrow found an extraordinary one in London at mid-century: the Crystal Palace built for the Great Exhibition of 1851. The earliest standardized building unit dated from several millennia before: the brick. It is easy to handle, it is delivered ready for use, its dimensions are constant, it permits a variety of patterns, and it does not require skilled labor. The Tower of Babel and Babylon's famous wall were made of brick. Along with stone, it built most of ancient Egypt. The use of standardized and prefabricated parts so that the only task at the site is to assemble them is the commonest modern practice. Thanks to new materials, it is also one of the most revolutionary. An initial success was scored by a man, mentioned earlier, who began life obscurely in an occupation remote from architecture: gardening.

Joseph Paxton was born in 1801 in Bedfordshire, England. He worked for the Horticultural Society in Chiswick. The Duke of Devonshire appointed him superintendent of his garden at Chatsworth—today twenty gardeners keep this historic place shipshape for the public. As early as 1837, he designed and erected the Chatsworth Conservatory, sixty-seven feet high, all metal bars and glass panes and all the same sizes and shapes. If an artist, sculptor, astronomer, and playwright could turn architect, so could a gardener. Out of his unique experience with standardized units, he designed one huge structure to house the entire Great Exhibition in Hyde Park. He built a single mammoth greenhouse three thousand feet long. It was a World's Fair under one roof.

Paxton's talent was narrowly channeled. He probably could not have worked with wood or brick, media unknown to him. Because of his conservatory at Chatsworth, he was familiar with all-glass walls and roofs supported by iron bars. They composed the Crystal Palace. Various manufacturers provided three thousand cast-iron columns and acres of glass. One drawing of one column sufficed for three thousand columns; one set of measurements for one pane did for all the panes; one machine, one mold in theory, could produce the entire building. In just six months there was bolted together a structure with an interior space four times that of St. Peter's in Rome—which had taken generations to construct. After three years the Hyde Park oddity was demounted easily and easily re-erected in Sydenham. It survived almost a hundred years before fire damaged it. Its sparkling surface helped Nazi planes orient themselves in World War II, and it had to be destroyed. But despite the absurdities of its appearance, it was recognized as a foretaste of a fabulous future. Queen Victoria knighted Paxton. For his last decade he served as member of Parliament from Coventry—a curious coincidence because this city has become the site of modern works as exciting and radical as Paxton's.

American business, envious of the success in London, gambled on a repeat show. Thus New York City got a baby Crystal Palace. The affair was staged in the former Reservoir Park. Now Bryant Park, it was between the old reservoir, where the Public Library stands, and the Avenue of the Americas. Paxton pioneered alone. It took two men here, neither one a gardener nor, properly speaking, an architect. They were Georg J. B. Carstensen and Charles Gildemeister. They erected the first cast-iron column—a symbol like laying the cornerstone—in October, 1852. Like all fairs, this started late. Like some true architects, the pair of backers blamed causes outside their control. They could have been right in one matter. Part of the task was detailed, accurate scheduling, in effect a traffic problem. Parts must arrive in the prescribed order and on time because this lot, like most urban lots, provided little extra ground for storage. Here the work area was cluttered with beams for the balcony before beams for the basement on which the balcony rested were delivered. A balcony was not like a brick wall; it could not start in mid-air.

The New York Crystal Palace, hardly a third as big as the overseas model, was flat, square-sided, and decorated with incongruous shapes. It looked as if someone were *going* to build, not as if someone had. The reservoir had a distinctly Egyptian air, like something along the Nile. No river anywhere jibed with the Crystal Palace. Across Forty-second Street rose the Latting Observatory, pointed, skeletal, a wood and metal forerunner of the Eiffel Tower in Paris. Most New Yorkers had their first elevator rides in one or the other of the local structures.

The public had to walk up and down the six floors of Paxton's palace. At the summit a huge arch marked the recessed entrance. At both catch-all exhibition halls, there were flags, bunting, drapes, fountains, lights, planting, and record-breaking crowds. Through the ages, builders had dreamed of walls to shield, protect, support, and also admit light. As if overnight, the combination of iron bar and glass offered exciting new prospects, though they came in odd-looking packages.

Paris boasted of its own Latting tower before the end of the century. But the boasting was buried at first under the attacks of some voluble foes. That pioneering construction illustrates the inflexible determination of the old to block the new, and the inflexible determination of the new not to be blocked. The builder was Alexandre Gustave Eiffel. As Paxton advanced from greenhouses to Crystal Palace, he advanced from bridges to the Eiffel Tower, the best known landmark in the capital.

Eiffel was born in Dijon in 1832. For several years he studied the mechanical arts and manufacturing. His work on the Paris fairs of 1867 and 1878 helped him to get his hand in for his major feat in 1889. Though he could not vie with the American James B. Eads or the Roeblings, engineers and bridge-builders, he turned out some masterful jobs like the Douro River Bridge in Portugal in 1877 and the Garabit viaduct in southern France in 1880-84. The former had a span of five hundred and thirty feet; the latter was even longer and higher. Americans may be most in his debt for the skeleton he designed for the Statue of Liberty in New York Harbor. His work with bridges prepared him for the Eiffel Tower—as the ribs of English ships held firm the church rooftree. The tower is bridge work run up straight in the air.

The Eiffel Tower is an even franker expression of modern materials than the Crystal Palace. Its nine thousand tons of iron are not decorated. It exerts the same direct and forthright impact as a sculptured abstraction. The four masonry feet beside the Seine River straddle about two and a half acres of land. It lines up splendidly with the huge Palais de Chaillot and its terraces and fountains on the opposite bank and with adjacent avenues—the French rarely miss the chance to add a vista to a façade or a façade to a vista. It is three hundred meters, or nine hundred and eighty-four feet high; a lantern crowns it; now a radio mast lifts it above one thousand feet. The four legs converge till, at a little over halfway up, they join forces for the rest of the dizzy rise. The lowest of three platforms is occupied by a restaurant. Separate elevators give the visitor three hair-raising lifts.

Is it ugly? Some angry contemporaries branded it as "useless" and "monstrous." They signed a manifesto. They deplored its shadow lying across their precious Paris like a smear of ink. "Suppose it lasts twenty years?" they demanded in dismay. Their fear has been more than realized. Today we qualify our agreement with those distinguished but shortsighted critics, among them the writer Guy de Maupassant and the composer Charles François Gounod. To millions who love Paris, the tower stands for Paris. Time has overlaid it with an ineffaceable sentimental patina. To find fault with it smacks of finding fault with the city it symbolizes. Here is a common difficulty: to judge not for values superimposed by the years and the emotions but absolutely, with extraneous considerations ruled out. The tower, theoretically, was an admirable engineering adventure. Aesthetically, it is not worth much. Neither is the Wright brothers' first plane, preserved in the Smithsonian Institute. To the architect, engineer, and historian, the Eiffel Tower is important. If public affection exaggerates its worth, the aesthete underrates it. They average out. A brave man thought it up and put it up. Man has always built hopefully, aspiringly toward the skies, as the pyramids and cathedrals bear witness. The Eiffel Tower, like the skyscraper about to appear in America, proved we still look upward.

At the same Paris fair of 1889, another building, inexcusably razed later, forecast the future more dramatically in some respects. Neither ornamental nor symbolic, it was, however, eminently practical. The touch of symbolism that saved the Eiffel might have saved it. It was the great Machinery Hall (Galerie des Machines). Metal arches soared high from hinged bases in the concrete floor. An area about five hundred by thirteen hundred feet was freed for displays.

The same city could boast of a traditional type of building boldly fashioned of untraditional material. The Ste.-Geneviève Library was iron; the architect was Théodore Labrouste, with whom America's architect, Henry Hobson Richardson, once worked.

The vast Halles Centrales, begun in 1853 to house a vast marketplace, was iron and glass. It has recently been doomed, as the market is to be removed from picturesque quarters in the heart of the city to a roomier site on the outskirts.

Modern materials also contributed to the most popular and spectacular kind of structure, an object of wonder even more than palace, cathedral, and skyscraper: the bridge. Two of the greatest bridges in the United States date from 1865 to 1875. Far apart—in New York City and St. Louis, Missouri—one was suspension and the other steel arch.

The wide-ranging ventures of James B. Eads included Army service, the salvage of sunken steamships, and the manufacture of glass in St. Louis. He devised an elaborate scheme, never put into effect, for a ship-railroad crossing from the Atlantic to the Pacific in mid-America. The route would have been via the isthmus of Tehuantepec, far south in Mexico, where talk about an interocean canal has been heard recently. His bridge, as good as ever, is still in use over the Mississippi River. It is known as the Eads Bridge. Grateful St. Louis, lucky in its heritage, puts up signs so the visitor can find it. Its three spans are each over five hundred feet long. They ride on flat arches that are dark, intriguing webs of tubular steel. Neither these hollow bars nor high-strength alloy steel had figured in bridge construction before, but they often did from then on.

This is a beautiful bridge. It is possible to make ungainly ones, like the angular skeletal form lately thrown across the Mississippi River at New Orleans. The 1,575-foot cantilevered central span, called the longest in the country, is an engineering feat. But grace and distinction are lacking. The long, low profile of the Eads Bridge reminds us more of jewelry than of engineering.

To some eyes, only the Roeblings' bridge across the East River in New York is more beautiful. John Augustus Roebling admired early suspension bridges in his native Germany. They suggest a hammock: a floor or roadway hangs beneath chains or cables strung from shore to shore. Roebling, equipped with a technical education and a degree, emigrated to this country. Near Pittsburgh, Pennsylvania, he established a factory for wire rope—substituted for hemp on the engine drums, this wound boats and cars up and down the inclines of the Portage Railroad, first to cross the Alleghenies into the Midwest. Roebling erected a wire-rope suspension aqueduct over the Allegheny River; the Monongahela suspension bridge at Pittsburgh; and several suspension aqueducts for the Delaware & Hudson Canal. Moving his factory to Trenton, New Jersey, he began in 1851 a major project: a suspension bridge at Niagara Falls. Contemporary engineers, perhaps jealous and certainly cynical, quickly voiced their doubts. The Niagara job stilled them all. Chains were replaced by Roebling's wire, and arch bridges gave way to suspension, thanks to his successes. In 1867, he engineered the longest span to date, 1,057 feet across the Ohio River at Cincinnati. Next he tackled his most challenging job. It cost him his life. At work on a tower for the Brooklyn Bridge, he was injured and died. The epochal structure was completed by his son, Washington Augustus Roebling, himself in part incapacitated by the long ordeal.

The Brooklyn Bridge is 5,989 feet long and has a central span of 1,595½ feet. Construction began in 1869; traffic was moving in 1883. Skeins of wire remind us of the handsome webs in St. Louis. The lines are simple, direct, and unforgettable. It is the one indisputable glory along a miserably neglected waterfront. Only in this century were longer suspension spans built. The several now around New York include the record-breaking Verrazano-Narrows Bridge, which we shall comment on later.

7 | Art and Architecture

Fairs like those in London, New York, and Paris call public attention to progress in numerous fields. They advertise architecture the most, however, for it houses the entire show. You cannot walk up and down every aisle, but you cannot help seeing walls, roofs, and grounds. A fair puts its best foot forward. It presents the workaday world in its Sunday best. There is a picture quality or Sunday-best quality to good architecture in and out of fairs. It is not only sound, modern, advanced building styles and methods; it is also conveniences, comforts, satisfactions, and looks.

In prehistory, man occupied a cave or crude shelter. Mud and grasses plastered on the sides and top of the shelter kept out some cold and rain. But architecture requires some art or the sign of some concern for art. A hint of it showed in the painting on the cave wall or in the designs on the skins the tepee was made of. The Museum of Modern Art in New York staged an exhibition, "Architecture Without Architects." It was architecture even without technical know-how because the builders tried for something more than a covering. They wanted a home rather than a house, a monument as well as a hall, an embellishment as well as a way to keep their feet dry in crossing a river.

When the trained architect steps on the scene, he wants not only a good-looking house but also a content or furnishings to match. With this in mind, we might date the modern movement from 1861. In that year, the firm of Morris, Marshall & Faulkner was founded in England. William Morris, the key instigator, crusaded for less copying and more originality in all creative fields. He suffered from an obsession about the machine. Convinced it could not produce art, he determined to revive the handicrafts. He advocated honesty in building, clean lines, and simple, practical design. Wallpaper, cloth, carpets, and furniture, including the Morris chair with its adjustable back, came from his workshop.

Perhaps we owe to him the first really modern house, built for and with Philip Webb. They did the entire job top to bottom, inside and out. As a further innovation, Morris used local materials like brick and roof tile. For lack of acceptable commercial furnishings, he made his own—chairs, tables, curtains, dishes. Thus the Webb house, product of a unified supervisory taste and mode, truly foreshadowed the modern approach.

Morris associated architecture with the practical arts. Across the channel, it was associated with art proper. The

interchange between the Old World and the New was frag-
mentary, although the idea of the Crystal Palace could sail
from London to New York. The interchange within Europe
was much more intimate. Architecture was more integrated
there and was consciously and purposefully linked with contemporary art. In America, the tendency is to compartmen-
talize and pigeonhole. Henry Hobson Richardson gave commissions here to sculptor Augustus Saint-Gaudens and
painter John La Farge. Nevertheless, the typical architect in
the United States fixed his attention more narrowly on architecture alone, without much consideration for art, as such.

Art Nouveau was New Art. So are all different and fresh
artistic endeavors. But this was new and timely and had an
influence on architecture. At the start, it claimed to be use-
ful. Eventually, it ignored utility, relapsed into overdecora-
tiveness, and petered out. It produced the elaborate Victor
Horta house in Brussels, with overfancy iron work and ornate scrolls weaving and winding across the wall. This is
paint-brush, not drawing-board, architecture.

The leading *Art Nouveau* architect, the Spaniard Antonio
Gaudi, worked in concrete. For him it was a fluid medium,
and he created fluid forms. Instead of being thick like batter,
his concrete seemed rather to pour like syrup. He did not
build; he sculptured. His constructions suggested Vincent
van Gogh's fiery and expressive paintings. It was a highly
personal, a sort of confessional, style. Gaudi laid bare the
inner secrets of Gaudi in his famous Casa Milá, the apartment building in Barcelona. This gingerbread fabrication or
confection might be an appropriate setting for Hansel and
Gretel.

Gaudi survived well into our century. The principal work
of his last years was the fantastic Sagrada Familia, or Holy
Family, Church in Barcelona. Nothing is straight that can be

curved, nothing plain that can be ornate. Carried to the extreme, this achieves an intensity or a frenzy of expression like that of Spanish and Mexican churrigueresque, a style in which not a square inch of surface is left without lavish sculpture. This intensity is religious and devout in its purpose and, to some eyes, in its effect. Some of this intimate urge to tell all worked itself out in the later Expressionism, a term used in the art world before it was adopted by architecture. The Expressionist painter was more interpretive than representational and more concerned to reveal himself than to do exact likeness. The Expressionist architect put up an office, house, or apartment vaguely resembling a military tank, Noah's Ark, or a trolley bus.

While *Art Nouveau* and Expressionism were far from the staid, worn past, they also lay outside the mainstream of modern architecture. Today architects tend to concentrate on form and structure and pay less heed than ever before to decoration. Some builders do away with it as much as possible. They eliminate, when they can, even seemingly essential elements that might be misconstrued as decorative. One, in a light mood, criticized plaster relief on a ceiling because looking at it, he complained, gave him a crick in the neck. But at bottom the objections were no joking matter. Adolf Loos, an Austrian, declared savagely, "Ornament is a crime."

8 | Henry Hobson Richardson

The first major exponent of twentieth-century styles appeared in the last half of the nineteenth. He reminds us of one of the structures we have been discussing: a bridge. A colossus, he planted one foot in the past and one in the future. With little of the engineer about him, he was indifferent to modern materials. Yet he possessed an independent, avant-garde attitude and the marvelous eye that is the sure sign of the profession. He is the American, Henry Hobson Richardson.

The stage was being set for pioneers of his interests and caliber. Engineers formed the American Society of Engineers in 1852. Some New York architects had a small-scale organization as early as 1803. The American Institute of Architects was founded in 1857. The first journal devoted to the profession was being published within a decade. Robert Mills, the first American specially trained as an architect, studied under a remarkable trio of teachers: Irish-born James Hoban, designer of the White House or the two White Houses, since he did the original and the second after the fire of 1814; Benjamin Henry Latrobe, the Englishman who led the Greek revival in the United States; and most notable of all, a president of the United States, Thomas Jefferson. In 1814, Jefferson drew up a revolutionary university curriculum that offered courses in architecture—the proposal could not be realized for years for lack of a competent teacher. Amateurs like Asher Benjamin gave drawing lessons. The Massachusetts Institute of Technology, Cornell, and the University of Illinois all had opened architectural schools by 1871. By the end of the century, three hundred and fifty venturesome pupils were studying this challenging subject in nine advanced institutions of learning.

Richardson was born on the Priestley plantation in the parish of St. James, Louisiana, in September, 1838. His home was named for his mother's grandfather, Joseph Priestley, a theologian but best remembered as the discoverer of oxygen. Young Richardson was graduated from Harvard in 1859. As a child in New Orleans he had studied art, and his goal was civil engineering. In Paris he applied for admission to the Ecole des Beaux-Arts. Of one hundred and twenty applicants, only sixty were accepted. The brilliant young American ranked eighteenth among them after the customary grueling month-long examinations. He settled in the Rue de Vaugirard in the Latin Quarter.

Life on the Left Bank had a Bohemian flavor. Richardson was in no mood to enjoy it. As he wrote to his fiancée in

Boston, "Study and society are incompatible." He bent diligently over his drawing board till late in the evening. Returning to Boston in 1862 in the midst of the Civil War, he was tempted to hurry on to his native state and enlist. A brother was fighting in the Confederate Army. Only a few years before, he himself had been cheated out of a military career at West Point because of his stammer. Though he did not go south, he was no Northern sympathizer and refused to take an oath of allegiance. These prickly circumstances drove him back to Paris—definitely to his benefit in the long run and definitely to ours.

His family had means, but war cut him off from their support and obliged him to earn his way. If Richard M. Hunt, the architect and brother of the painter William Morris Hunt, was the first American at the Beaux-Arts, Richardson was the second. This was a mark of distinction in Paris and, coupled with his obvious talent, helped him to find work. Though he wore expensive suits he had bought in London, the pockets were sometimes empty in Paris. His stammer seems not to have handicapped him. A personable fellow, fond of company, he was a chess player and an amateur flutist. Tall, broad-shouldered, deep-chested, he had brown eyes, a dark complexion, and dark hair parted in the middle. When later he ranked as the leader in his field in the United States, an admiring Dutchman detected a monumental look about him, as though he resembled his own buildings.

He spent one night in jail. The French government ill-advisedly tried to impose on the Beaux-Arts faculty a professor of its choosing, Viollet-le-Duc. He was an eminent medievalist and author. The students did not have a case against him, but they did have against the government and paraded in protest. Quite a few were arrested, among them Richardson. By good luck he shared a cell with a well-known romantic author, Théophile Gautier. Officials finding them together in the morning freed them both.

The general aspect of France and Paris might have educated Richardson as much as specific courses. A walk about that incomparable capital was bound to develop a sharper eye and a more exacting taste. As an observer has pointed out, there was a good lesson for him to learn at the Opéra. Jean Louis Charles Garnier, one-time Beaux-Arts student, built it during the reign of Napoleon III. It is overfancy and over-decorated. A long wide avenue rises to it and ends at it. The vista is as splendid as at the Eiffel Tower. It is an extravagant picture framed by a square simplified and standardized —façades the same height and design. This restrained setting tones down the extravagance; conversely, the plainness is relieved by the ornate opera house. Richardson would decorate, too, but would know where to stop—a mark of the great architect as well as the great painter.

Architects in his day did not regard their task as an invitation to originality or ingenuity. Instead of trying to think up something different, they chose an antique style guaranteed respectable by the roll of the centuries. Then they simply copied it. If they liked the Greek, as Latrobe did, they pitched the roofs low and supported them on rows of pillars as in Athens, Paestum, and other sacred Mediterranean sites. If they liked Gothic, they pointed up the doors and windows of their churches. Outside, they stuck on skimpy versions of the flying buttresses, appendages as useless now as an appendix to a human being, but which served in their period to keep slender walls from buckling beneath a heavy roof. Jefferson used the Maison Carrée, the jewel of Nîmes in southern France—a Roman temple modeled on a Greek temple—as the model for the Virginia State Capitol, which he designed. The same faultless structure later modeled for the Madeleine Church in Paris. It is handsomer in the original than in the oversize version in the French capital. Hoban's White House was a Georgian mansion transported from England to the Potomac.

Richardson's choice fell on Romanesque. With its round arches and massive walls, it was characterized by a sense of weight and substance. It was monumental, as Richardson was credited with being in the flesh and the spirit. The modern observer also felt the tangy breath of the romantic implied by the name. But instead of copying slavishly, Richardson merely used the style, bending it to his own fresh purposes. He was not building churches that could be classified as Romanesque, like St. Gilles and Moissac. No one ever could again. He did a church or two, but his chief assignments were railroad stations and banks, a courthouse, a jail, and a department store. To twentieth-century ends he masterfully adapted a manner eight or nine centuries old.

All about him there was a spate of second-rate work. The professional often designed handsomely in order to attract a client and built cheaply to clear the maximum profit. What Richardson said on the drawing board was what he, in fact, conscientiously carried out. He was a superior draftsman. His biographer, Henry-Russell Hitchcock, believes few contemporaries produced such rapid and revealing sketches.

In 1865, with peace restored to the United States, he returned to New York, his headquarters for a decade. Most of his commissions then and later were for clients in New England, Chicago, and Pittsburgh. Clients were easy to find, too, luckily, for the novice architect has no tougher nut to crack —much tougher than for the writer, painter, or composer. A painter may spend a week, a month, a year—one contemporary spends three to five years—on a single canvas. His expenses are his living, paints, brushes, studio rent, model's fee, but no more. Pen, pencil, and paper for book or musical composition do not put anyone into debt. If a man devotes a year to a symphony, an opera, or a novel, only his own time and basic costs are lost if the music is never performed and the story never published. The case in architecture is vastly different. For even a small house, the client must write checks for the design, the drawings, the labor and materials, and the price of the land. If he hires someone without experience, who can guarantee the house will stand up, keep out the weather, be heatable, and last for a year, a generation? The cheapest house Richardson built cost $2,500, cheap then and even cheaper now, adjusting to the present dollar value. Still it was a risk for the buyer. Suppose we had in mind a church, a railroad station, a store. Would we choose a man who had never built one before? Would we pass out even to an experienced architect without serious qualms the $50,000 or $200,000 or the larger sum demanded by major construction? Since the stakes are greater than in any other creative line, clients are proportionately harder to sign up.

Competitions tempt the architect, though he enters them more and more reluctantly. He must draw up extensive plans. He may have to meet draftsmen's salaries for weeks. If the winner alone is compensated for his effort and office expenses, few beginners can afford to play the game. Richardson loved such gambles, however. They helped secure him several commissions. One was for the great Brattle Street Church in Boston; another for the Hampden County Courthouse in Springfield, Massachusetts, both still standing. In 1870, he won in two of three competitions. But despite his self-confidence and the wonderful promise of his Paris record, he could not at first be sure of a welcome for his theoretical but untested talent. This uncertainty wears down the stoutest heart. He was anxious for the Unitarian Church job on State Street in Springfield—it is now demolished. The trustees made him wait. When he heard they had decided in his favor, he burst into tears.

One of his virtues—in this respect following Morris's example—was his frank exploitation of local stone. Large blocks of it went into the F. L. Ames gate lodge in North Easton, Massachusetts. Longmeadow stone was used in the Springfield church.

Though an alien style was his starting point, he badgered it, fought it, and shaped it into his own and our own. The sense of Romanesque scale is preserved in the smallest structures his society required of him. His Emmanuel Church in what was Allegheny City and is now part of Pittsburgh was commissioned in 1883. The small, admirably simple building had a steeply pitched roof and eaves that dropped down almost to the ground. The brick of the façade matched the sidewalk. Three steps climbed to three low-arched entrances. Here was the dark, compact, sturdy look of the Old World. Designed today, it would receive and deserve the enthusiastic praise of ultra-moderns.

His $2,500 house for a minister in Marion, Massachusetts, has been called one of our "vital monuments." Mansions, courthouses, and capitols are easy. The small and intimate house is the ultimate test. Monumental edifices serve about the same ceremonial purpose today as a thousand or two thousand years ago. Houses are private, particular, and more related to their times than other structures. The United States Senate could meet in the Roman Senate. An American family would probably wind up cold, hungry, sore, and sleepless in the kind of house whose remains now gape open on the ancient Forum. Though Richardson worked on plenty of large-scale buildings, the Marion house, shingled, wood-framed, with recessed porches, surely called out the best in him. The gambrel roof cut by small dormer windows dropped down low, like a visor, as on the Pittsburgh church. This helped set the fashion for the cottages that multiplied in New England and the East until well into this century.

On the Albany (New York) State Capitol, Richardson was associated with his friend Frederick Law Olmsted of Central Park fame. His Sever Hall at Harvard was finished in 1880. The roof was handsomely broken up with fine low dormers and squat heavy chimneys. In front were two rounded, slightly protruding bays. Above the arched entrance there rose, in low relief, in effect, the façade of a two-story house with gable. Two shallow decorative slabs set off the rear entrance. The building in brick, handled in the grand manner, was new in spirit and yet, thanks to Richardson's sensitive eye, did not clash with old forms jostling it on the university campus.

Richardson regarded the courthouse and jail in Pittsburgh, still happily standing, and the Marshall Field store in Chicago as his best works. The seven-story store contained some metal in interior beams and piers. The walls, though thinned down considerably, were masonry and supporting. The double windows between the piers in the first three stories were then reduced to one and topped off with a row of smaller ones. Commissioned in 1885, this kept Richardson busy in the last year of his life.

His practice on occasion required the employment of twenty men. His fee was five percent of the cost plus travel expenses, for a total of about eight percent. Among other apprentices in his office were Charles McKim and Stanford White. Louis Sullivan studied him to advantage. Thus it was partly through Sullivan as intermediary that Richardson's originality, independence, and pioneering vision were passed on to Frank Lloyd Wright and were fed into the present and future of American architecture.

He was not, however, a modernist in any literal sense. Just as his memorable career reached its climax, ways of raising skyscrapers higher than any around, even today, were developed. They interested him little. Despite his engineering training, he was not concerned with technical problems or with what may have seemed the peculiar, perhaps mistaken, interest of his colleagues in the potential of metal. His hand, like Morris's, was trained in the past; his eye looked to the future.

Prospective clients were warned bluntly before any contract was signed that they would acquire a good building, but it would not necessarily please them or strike them as handsome. Then Richardson went ahead and did his superb best. Like Morris, he designed furniture and appurtenances. Leading sculptors and painters beautified his constructions. He was never sure how a house, store, or office would turn out till the last lick of work was done. As he explained, "The architect acts on his building, but his building reacts on him —helps to build itself." Chary of decoration anywhere, he was particularly stingy with it on the exterior. Moldings and stone courses stayed flat so that no dirt gathered to form black lines and splotches on his harmonious façade.

When he appeared on the scene, the Gothic style dominated architecture. French Romanesque, as in his Trinity Church in Boston, became popular, especially in the fast-growing Midwest. It gave way, unfortunately, to Roman classicism following the Columbian Exposition in Chicago in 1893. Richardson's Romanesque would have served our scene infinitely better than the Exposition's "safe" classicism.

9 | Louis H. Sullivan

Louis H. Sullivan was one American—Frank Lloyd Wright another—who saw no crime in decoration. Sullivan was our first modernist. He built our first true skyscraper, the Wainwright Building in St. Louis, Missouri, true in looks, spirit, and form. It may also be our handsomest. Though he might have regretted his achievement if he were alive now, he, in effect, endowed New York with its world-famous skyline. Scores of high-flying cities in many countries derive from him. His answer to the problems of overcrowding and prohibitive land costs was not perfect but the only one generally accepted.

He came at the right time—unless the time was right because he came. Iron, steel, and glass were waiting. A more practical means of anchoring buildings in Chicago's slippery subsoil had been developed. Nowadays piers are sunk a hundred feet to rock or hardpan, and watertight walls enclose basements. The elevator was powered by electricity in 1880.

Sullivan's father, born in Ireland, founded a dancing academy in London. In 1847, he sailed by steerage to the New World and Boston, where he founded another dancing school. Here he married Andrienne Françoise List, daughter of impoverished Swiss parents from Geneva. The son of this immigrant fiddler-dancer and Andrienne, born in 1856, had a haphazard upbringing. From the age of five on, his fiddler-dancer father turned him over to his Swiss grandparents on their farm in South Reading, Massachusetts. There he spent his summers till he was fourteen. After his parents had moved to Chicago, he settled in South Reading and commuted to school in Boston. His *Autobiography* draws a lively picture of the formative years. The steady swing of the long-handled broom of the street sweeper impressed on him a sense of rhythm. He learned about craftsmanship from a cobbler. The bursting of the make-believe dam in a brook taught him something about power. Starry notions of romance blossomed out of the Irish tales told him by the hired girl on the farm.

He devoted hour after hour to the same sort of watchful walk as ours at the start of this book. Buildings of all kinds were catalogued in his memory of Boston. He reported of them, "Some said vile things, some said prudent things .,. . but none said noble things." He had not then read, because it had not been written, *Dialogues* by the Frenchman Paul Valéry. A Valéry character, a Greek philosopher, remarks that buildings resemble people: some are mute, some speak, and still others sing.

An incident on one of Sullivan's rambles guided him into his life work. At the Masonic Temple—which he presumably felt "said vile things"—he caught a glimpse of his first architect. This "large and dignified" person, he would report, was bearded and wore a "top hat and frock coat." He crossed the sidewalk, stepped into a fine carriage, and was driven off. The sight overwhelmed the schoolboy. If that represented the architect, if that was the status an architect acquired, Sullivan determined there and then to become one. He enrolled in the Massachusetts Institute of Technology's young school, but it bored him. In accordance with the inevitable academic routine, he had to study ancient styles and copy the architectural orders. They did not interest him then or ever. One year in college was all he could stand. The reputation of Richard Morris Hunt drew him straightaway to New York. But Hunt with endless stories of student days at the Beaux-Arts in Paris also bored him. He moved on to Philadelphia.

How could a stranger find a good architect? Find a good building. The building that intrigued him was by Frank Furness, who gave him a job. But in the depression of 1873, the last hired was the first fired. Sullivan had been aiming for Chicago. Now he joined his parents there. Wide areas of the lakeside city had vanished in the dreadful flames of 1871. Buildings to replace them were in urgent demand. Drawing boards were covered with plans. Again as in Philadelphia, he searched for a building he liked and asked for work with its architect. The proof of his advanced outlook, taste, and sense of the future lies in the quality of the man to whom he applied: William Le Baron Jenney, an arrogant, tough fighter, an engineer rather than architect, and a man curious about this new material, cast iron.

Despite his impatience with education, Sullivan did not stay long with Jenney. Education deserved another try, he decided, and he sailed for Paris. Skirting his father's birthplace, the ship landed him at Liverpool. He wandered around London for two weeks. Renting a room in the Latin Quarter in Paris, he passed those difficult Beaux-Arts examinations. As a student in the atelier Vaudremer, a studio for practice and study, he was again set to copying the classical orders. So he played truant on invaluable trips to Florence and Rome. For the second time, it was no trouble to persuade himself he had had enough formal education. The Beaux-Arts, though he criticized it later, taught him something about composition and logic. One of his little vanities in after years was to pretend his stay in Europe lasted longer than the actual six months.

Iron and steel were discussed learnedly as the building materials of the future. Phrases like "structural realism" and "rational building" were in the air. Sullivan studied engineering. He read about the Eads Bridge going up in St. Louis. But he read outside his immediate field: Ralph Waldo Emerson, Edmund Spenser, Shakespeare, and Walt Whitman. He met another man who was an engineer in the Civil War: Dankmar Adler. The famous Adler & Sullivan firm was founded in Chicago in 1881.

The first efforts by this team were a bit capricious and fanciful. Instead of letting a building speak for itself, they kept breaking up its surfaces and profile. It did not speak; it jabbered. The roof line was determinedly irregular. The façade was marred by protuberances and recessions, by bumps and hollows. Oriel and bay windows and gables were

Louis Sullivan: *The Wainwright Building*, St. Louis, Missouri.
   [*Courtesy, Downtown in St. Louis, Inc., and Winfrey Studio*]

ABOVE   Frank Lloyd Wright: *Fallingwater,* Bear Run, Pennsylvania.
   [*Photo by Paul Mayen, courtesy, Western Pennsylvania Conservancy*]

RIGHT   Frank Lloyd Wright: *The Solomon R. Guggenheim Museum,* New York City.
   [*Courtesy, The Solomon R. Guggenheim Museum*]

ABOVE   Frank Lloyd Wright: Interior, *The Solomon R. Guggenheim Museum,* New York City.

[*Courtesy, The Solomon R. Guggenheim Museum*]

TOP RIGHT   Le Corbusier: *Villa Stein,* Garches, France, seen from the garden.

[*Courtesy, The Museum of Modern Art, New York*]

BOTTOM RIGHT   Le Corbusier: *Notre Dame du Haut,* Ronchamp, France.

[*Courtesy, French Cultural Services*]

LEFT   Le Corbusier: *Swiss Pavilion,* University City, Paris.
[*Courtesy, French Cultural Services*]

BELOW   Richard J. Neutra: *Corona School,* Bell, California.
[*Photo by Julius Shulman, courtesy, Richard J. Neutra*]

Pier Luigi Nervi: *George Washington Bridge Bus Station,* New York City
—with George Washington Bridge in left background.
   [*Courtesy, The Port of New York Authority*]

all appliquéd not for the sake of light but looks. The effect was not quiet but noisy.

Sullivan learned how to anchor a structure in the squashy subsoil of Chicago. Such matters as light, heat, and traffic— that is, movement along corridors and stairs—were within his province. In particular, he adapted iron to the tall building. It is not easy to change from one method to another, one potential to another. Old-style wall construction consisted of solids. Now the architect worked, so to speak, with holes or frames or skeletons. The strength was in the edges, and in between he needed only fill. For Sullivan, iron did not imitate conventional materials; it acted and appeared and behaved like iron. By an extension of this, he also tried to make the building look its size.

The firm's first major success was the Chicago Auditorium, opened formally in 1889. It was a technical triumph, though not wholly an aesthetic one. The two men could do whatever they wished but could not guarantee it would look well when done. Besides the Auditorium with 4,200 seats, the project included a hotel and business offices. Adler handled technical problems such as acoustics—he was a consultant on New York's Carnegie Hall. The house floor sloped. Machinery was stashed away beneath the stage. The inside was constructed of cast-iron columns, but outside walls of brick bore the full burden. The handsome Auditorium owed its compact, substantial, restrained appearance in part to Richardson's Romanesque.

Adler had one odd problem that demanded an ingenious solution. The complex of walls and offices rested on a continuous all-around foundation. As the walls were raised evenly, it was figured they would sink evenly to their eventual level in the tricky subsoil. A hefty tower was to surmount one section. To add it at the end of the operation would force that section down disproportionately low. So as the section rose, Adler piled extra loads on it temporarily so that it had sunk to its ultimate correct position when the tower was erected.

Though Sullivan's career lay in the city, he took the country as his guide and inspiration. The South Reading farm left its mark on Chicago and St. Louis. A building, in his opinion, should have a form like a tree, not the shape of one but its naturalness and inevitability. Like a tree it should grow. His phrase for the process by which, in effect, the structure built itself was, "The function of a building must organize its form." He shortened this in 1895 to three words: "Form follows function." All modern architecture in all lands subscribes to this without reservation. So did great architecture in the past. A building is not modern unless form follows function. Indeed it is not then a building at all but a plaything or a fantasy.

Sullivan believed creation was not reasoned or logical but intuitive, and he mistrusted "rational principles and formulas." The environment must be reflected in the building. The building must "look like what it is" and be what it looks like. Ornament must belong, that is, harmonize with basic forms and materials. His *Kindergarten Chats,* as he entitled them, expressed ideas with a pithiness beyond the understanding of kindergartners. Though he occasionally rang in a "go to," "forsooth," or "avaunt," he had a vivid and persuasive vocabulary. He advised a young man, "Strive not, I caution you, after what is called originality." Of the Wainwright skyscraper we credit him with, he pointed out: "The sixteen-story building must not consist of sixteen separate, distinct, and unrelated buildings piled one upon the other until the top of the pile is reached." Sullivan dismissed schools of architecture with, "A plague on them." One of his derisive comments in a world of copycats was, "The Roman temple can no more exist on Monroe Street, Chicago, U.S.A., than can Roman civilization exist there."

Frank Lloyd Wright worked with or for this ticklish and unpredictable genius on important commissions, as we shall see. The younger man, a genius no less ticklish and unpredictable, knew his mentor intimately. Sullivan often had some botany textbook with him. He took the time to read a paragraph aloud and expatiate on natural form as the proper model. In Wright's admiring recollection, Sullivan was a "small brown man of aristocratic bearing, with a number of sharp pencils on his desk and an equally pointed glance." He paid Wright $25 a week when he first came to work and esteemed him so highly that, in effect, he hired an understudy for him, which proved to be a sensible precaution.

Wright relates an incident that reminds us of Richardson. A woman who came to Sullivan for a Colonial house was informed bluntly, "Madame, you will take what we give you."

Wright particularly praised specific features of the Auditorium Sullivan designed: the spacious, well-placed corridors and the banquet hall, which technically was a building hung inside the bigger building. In the Auditorium tower, Adler & Sullivan opened new offices. There Wright the novice listened for hours to the talkative Sullivan. The apprentice dedicated to his calling was extremely impressionable. He was every bit as smitten with Sullivan's appearance and manner as Sullivan had been with the gentleman proceeding to his carriage in Boston. Wright credited Sullivan with a "haughty air"; noted that he never condescended to bid his staff good morning; and found fault with his walk for its "dangerous resemblance to a strut." This may have been unfair—unless

Wright meant to be laudatory, in which case it was unde-
served. Richardson had had a stammer; Sullivan, too, had a
physical defect: a bad hip caused a slight limp.

Sullivan's next important contribution to our architecture
was his contribution to the 1893 Columbian Exposition in
Chicago. The architect Daniel Burnham had charge of the
big lake-front fair. If Burnham's partner, the more liberal
John Wellborn Root, or Henry Hobson Richardson had been
alive, the architecture on that historic occasion would have
been less dull and derivative. Wright attacked the event as a
"disaster." Sullivan declared the fair had done enough damage to last half a century. This was not much of an exaggera-
tion. Over acre after acre, the buildings were uninspired,
banal copies—with one exception.

Burnham invited Easterners to help. The outsiders—Richard M. Hunt, Charles Follen McKim, William R. Mead, and
Stanford White—were good men. But their ideas dated from
five or ten centuries earlier, and they were no prophets of the
morrow. Burnham inexcusably ignored the progressives busy
at his elbow boosting Chicago to top place architecturally.
The fair promoted the construction of unified and harmonious building groups, Burnham argued with some
justification. But the total lack of vision dismayed all those
dreaming of a better world. Many state exhibits were housed
in copies of copies of copies. The over-all design was based
on the absurd assumption that nothing served the future so
well as models exhumed from the dead past. There were
replicas of Boston's John Hancock House, an old mission,
Mount Vernon, and a part of Philadelphia's Independence
Hall. Among assorted styles were Gothic, Renaissance, Eliz-
abethan, Islamic, Colonial, and Georgian. It may have been
historical; it was not architectural.

One outstanding construction was recognized at once by

informed visitors as the grand prize winner. It was the Transportation Building from the workshop of Adler & Sullivan. Wright helped with it. The major virtue was that it was different. It rejected the worn and tedious classicism imported from the proper Eastern seaboard by the borrowed architects. It was, instead, new, vital, vigorous. It challenged the past and saluted the future. Not one Greek column was plastered on it. It was big, square, and plain. The chief feature was the golden door. Its vast florid pattern offered a breath-taking relief from the formal drabness all about. Here, it proclaimed to the public, is the exciting frame to the exciting entrance to exciting exhibits. If there were Beaux-Arts touches, they may have helped persuade French jurors to award it three medals. On the whole, it testified to independent and progressive thinking. When all else on the fairgrounds faded from the mind's eye, this stayed bright.

If any one work of Sullivan's assures him his position in history, it was the Wainwright Building in St. Louis. Erected for a wealthy brewer, Ellis Wainwright, by great good fortune it is still standing. It faces a street packed much of the day with autos creeping toward a nearby parking space. Most notable at first glance is its color—color in a skyscraper, which until then had mostly been dull, flat gray. In that building, Sullivan used rich red granite, brown sandstone, red brick, and red terra cotta for a broad, brilliant frieze to top it off. The granite gives the Wainwright a spirited lift of a couple of feet off the sidewalk. Next come two floors of sandstone. Above them rise handsome brick piers clear to the tenth story. We need no special training at all to identify this as a masterpiece. Besides, it is the first of its kind. We are lucky to have the testimony of Frank Lloyd Wright:

"Our peculiar invention, the skyscraper, began on our soil when Louis H. Sullivan came through the door that connected my little cubicle with his room in the Auditorium tower, pushed a drawing board with a stretch of manila paper upon it over onto my table.

"There it was, in delicately pencilled elevation. I stared at it and sensed what had happened. It was the Wainwright Building—and there was the very first human expression of a tall steel office building as architecture. It was tall and consistently so—a unit, where all before had been one cornice building on top of another cornice building. This was a greater achievement than the Papal dome, I believe." Wright ridiculed the famous dome. To prevent its tremendous weight from spreading the walls it rested on, Michelangelo bound it with a huge chain. In Wright's opinion this was a confession of failure, for the dome itself should contain its own stresses.

The Wainwright is a gem. If a building can be lovable, this is lovable. The walls of the Auditorium and tower in Chicago were decorated unnecessarily, as if walls by themselves could not possess superlative qualities. The Auditorium was a mixture of large and small windows alternately arched and flat, a four-story tier and a two-story, windows in pairs and then in threesomes. The eye moved up but was arbitrarily stopped. It moved horizontally and was stopped again. The eye insists on the freedom to roam, but here nothing moved, or nothing moved smoothly. As Gaudi was too fluid, this was too jerky. Someone complained that the Auditorium was not one building but a series of different buildings each with separate top and bottom, set on one another or intersecting one another. Paxton's Crystal Palace in standardized bar and glass had too little variety. The Auditorium had too much. The Wainwright can be criticized. The corner piers are thick—but are not the corner pillars on the Parthenon praised for being intentionally thickened? Piers bearing weight are not differentiated from those that simply serve as window frames or mullions. But the entire structure possesses a magnificent verticality. It lifts, and it lifts us with it. The windows are set back slightly, and an interesting pattern of light and shadow shifts across the spandrels, the sections of wall between the top of one window and the bottom of the window above it. As one proof of the soundness of the design, the shiny modernized entrances do not detract from the total effect.

Asked to do a bank for a small Midwest city, Sullivan reported at the site dutifully. For a couple of days he stood or sat on a curbstone to get the lay of the land, the look of the surroundings, the traffic density, and so on Then he handed in his design and an estimate of the cost. One stuffy director regretted there was not a row of columns. At once Sullivan rolled up his sketch. Plenty of architects but never Louis H. Sullivan could do columns, he said, bowing out. He was awarded the commission. The eventual cost was within $1,000 of his first figure.

Between 1880 and 1895, he turned out more than a hundred buildings. In the almost thirty years that were left to him, he did only twenty. His life fell apart miserably. He was a hard man to deal with. He was set in his ideas and sometimes offensively uncompromising. Clients who dared suggest even minor changes in design met with harsh and impolitic refusals. There were serious domestic troubles. The panic of 1893 resulted in the dissolution of the partnership with Adler. The facile successes of some associates embittered him. He lost the shingled house with miniature tower and deep porch that he designed and built for vacations in Ocean Springs, Mississippi. One by one his draftsmen walked out. His art collection and fine furniture were auctioned off to help pay his debts. His living quarters changed from the elegant Chicago Club to a wretched hotel. Finally in 1918, he was forced out of his offices in the Auditorium tower. From 1919 until his death in 1924, he had only one small commission: a small façade for a small shop.

The unique Sullivan stamp is still to be noted in two other places. One was the Bayard, or Condict, Building in downtown New York. It is a shame that the designer of the true skyscraper was represented by only one work in the skyscraper capital. The other outstanding job was a Chicago department store, originally Schlesinger & Mayer, better known as Carson Pirie Scott & Company. Provided at first with a bit of a cornice, the top was eventually sheared off even with the wall. Windows were set almost flush with it. Verticals fixed in the corner spotted the admirable entrance. Horizontals streamed off from it left and right—and there was another of Sullivan's beautiful surfaces. Thanks to the steel frame, extra room was freed for counters and aisles. But the building commanded attention mostly for exterior perfections. Fine iron work ornamented the bottom two stories. Passers-by headed automatically for the entrance. Window space for displays was generous and handsomely arranged. The corner, with its superb fit into the body of the building, was one of Sullivan's triumphs. This transition from one shape to another, from one quality of container to another, tests a builder's taste and wit drastically. The towers of Old World cathedrals are the classic examples. In how few of them do the four sides of the tower manage to slip gracefully and smoothly into the six sides of the mounting spire!

Sullivan's work days neared an end. He still remained the fighter for modernity and the fiery critic. He indignantly condemned the Chicago Tribune Tower competition jury for giving the prize, and the job, to Raymond Hood and Gothic when it should have gone to the fresh and vigorous design of a Finn named Eliel Saarinen. If he could not build, he could still instruct the younger men with his *Kindergarten Chats*. The leader of that upcoming generation was Frank Lloyd Wright. Sullivan's debt to Frank Lloyd Wright could be as great as Wright's to him.

Whether we are interested in modern architecture in the United States, Japan, South America, or Europe, whether the periods important to us are the closing half of the last century or the opening half of this, we run repeatedly into Frank Lloyd Wright. Despite personal failings coupled with professional faults, he came closer than anyone to being the ubiquitous, dominant master builder of his day. A long day it was, too. He lived a span of time as extraordinary as the spans the nearly omnipotent architect can now erect. His shadow falls across three generations. Or his light has guided three generations. It will guide more.

For ten years in the middle of his meteoric and in spots

lurid career, when all the professionals were familiar with his name, he did not earn enough to keep the sheriff from his door. Wisconsin was his birthplace. Both there and in Arizona, he built beautiful homes the two states brag about shamelessly. Neither state ever awarded him one commission. The United States government, which employs an army of architects for post offices, embassies, military installations, and warehouses, never asked him for so much as a sentry box. New York City can count only two buildings signed by Wright. One, the Mercedes-Benz showroom, amounted to little more than an interior remodeling. The other, the Solomon R. Guggenheim Museum, testifies to his amazing versatility—he may be compared to Pablo Picasso, the painter, who also has many strings to his bow. It is a virtuoso performance. Granted that it attracts his fans by the thousands, it does not fulfill too well its assigned function.

New York's neglect may not be surprising because Wright was not a city fellow. Though he worked in Chicago, Tokyo, Buffalo, Racine, and many other populous centers, he was a country boy. Architecture is fundamentally an urban activity. Yet in his opinion, "The land is the simplest form of architecture." No one in our time was blessed with his sixth sense for fitting a building to its site, spreading it out on the prairie, nestling it among the trees, or clamping it fast to a steep hillside as though it had always belonged there. In this feeling for physical kinship, he has no peer. He tucked his houses in. The roof reached out cosily over the wall edges. It seemed to draw closer to the ground. It tried to protect the exposed flanks not only from rain and snow but also from every threat.

He had a head start over most professionals. He was not allowed to wait for boyhood, or even infancy, to enter on his career. Before he was born, his mother set her heart on a son and an architect. In keeping with a then current belief, she conscientiously conditioned him prenatally, as she supposed, by feasting her eyes on pictures of historic monuments. Even his toys were selected by this determined woman in order to direct him toward not necessarily his but her chosen profession. Our parents and grandparents called these toys Fröbel blocks. These maple blocks, smooth and agreeably colored, could be arranged as walls or houses or whatever the youngster fancied. Wright's father interested him in literature and music. On a future day he would salute as the greatest of all architects the composers Bach and Beethoven. Within his own sphere, however, he promoted himself to the head of the class. He never hid his light under a bushel. He set out to be in his words "the greatest architect who ever lived." Examining the design of a colleague, he once exclaimed with biting humor, "What a great architect—I am!"

William Russell Cary Wright, his father, a music teacher, was a widower when he met Anna Lloyd-Jones. She was the daughter of a Welshman with a variety of talents: farmer, hatmaker, and lay preacher. The budding genius, her son Frank Lloyd Wright, was only seven or eight when she gave him the potent Fröbel blocks. He would remember, "Those blocks stayed in my fingers all my life."

After a short while at a private school in Massachusetts, the curly-headed boy returned to a public school in Madison, Wisconsin. Like other youngsters, he spent his spare time on a bobsled or iceboat, and he also made a crossbow. Life was wonderful—until all of a sudden it was transformed into hardship. His volatile father walked out of the house, and no Wright or Lloyd-Jones laid eyes on him again. A two-part problem now dropped heavily on the slim sixteen-year-old shoulders: he must help support the family as well as acquire the education he and his mother longed for. Thanks to Allen

D. Conover, a contractor who doubled as head of engineering at the University of Wisconsin, he was able to continue his studies and earn money in Conover's office. Descriptive geometry may have been valuable. The other class work seemed fruitless, and during his sophomore year he quit. No architecture as such was ever taught him formally. Quite a few architects today, like most of them in the past, are self-trained. Richardson's background was more rounded than Wright's, and Sullivan's considerably richer. But Wright was a reader and a thinker, or at least a theorizer. Books were always within reach. One favorite author, John Ruskin, left one important lesson with him: building was a moral as well as a technical and aesthetic affair. That is, a piece of work could be honest or dishonest, look like what it was and what it was made of or be a fake.

When Wright was elected to a fraternity at the university, his mother met the added expense by pawning a gold watch. For his first college dance, she found a mink collar to sew on his overcoat. All his life he was surrounded by worshipers like this almost too-devoted woman who shielded him from personal and professional criticism.

One dramatic and formative experience in Madison was extracurricular and due to chance. An essay of his describes it excitedly—he was a breathless writer. As he was passing the new wing of the State Capitol . . .

"Suddenly I heard the roar of collapse—saw the clouds of white lime-dust rise high in the air—heard the groans and fearful cries of those injured and not killed—some forty workmen dead or seriously hurt . . . sick with horror as men plunged headlong from the basement openings—some seeming to be still madly fighting off falling bricks and timbers, only to fall dead in the grass outside, grass no longer green but whitened by the big falling clouds of lime— Stone basement piers carrying the iron interior supporting columns had given way and the roof took all the floors, sixty men at work on them, clear down to the basement. A great 'classic' cornice had been projecting boldly out from the top of the building, against the sky. Its moorings partly torn away, this cornice now hung down in place, great hollow bones of galvanized iron, hanging up there suspended on end. One great section of cornice I saw hanging above an upper window. A workman hung head downward, his foot caught, crushed on the sill of this window, by a falling beam . . ."

He remembered angrily "the spectacle of that sham feature [the cornice] hanging there, deadly menace to the pitifully moaning, topsy-turvy figure of a man—a workingman . . ." About this "empty sheet-iron" fake, he reflected that it merely pretended to be stone. What was worse, it put on this pretense as an element of "the Capitol of the great state of Wisconsin . . . what a shame!" Here was dishonesty in Ruskin's sense. Wright was never guilty of a cornice real or bogus. The cornice and its uselessness became the subject of a Wright lecture and paper.

His mother urged him to continue his studies at Wisconsin. What he most needed, he was convinced, was practical, paying experience in an office. His books and the mink collar brought in $7 at a pawnshop. That paid for a railroad ticket and left a little change. With his belongings in a carpetbag, he sallied forth to the assault of Chicago. It was 1887; he was eighteen.

Though it is cruel to say so, Chicago's calamitous fire benefited Wright as it had Sullivan. The stricken city even *wanted* raw youngsters with little education and experience. To begin with, fate perhaps tested him with a short nagging wait. Before he grew disheartened, he landed his first job as a tracer with Joseph Lyman Silsbee. His pay was $8 a week.

Compared to his exaggerated but emphatic idea of his worth, this was a pittance. He pestered his boss for $12. Then he asked for $15. When that was refused, he resigned to work for another firm. The new job did not suit him. When he returned, Silsbee peered over the top of his gold-rimmed glasses. "Here you are again, eh?" he said. "You may have $18."

Silsbee's was only a way station. Wright soon recognized the ideal employer: Louis Sullivan, with whom he shared a bit of a Massachusetts background. Sullivan became his employer, counselor, friend, and "beloved master." Sullivan, in turn, justly appreciated the raw, astute, and ambitious youngster from Madison.

Wright's rapid advance aroused the jealousy of older draftsmen. The threat of trouble was too clear for Wright to ignore. He did not smoke or drink. To save carfare and also to harden his muscles, he walked eighty blocks a day to and from work. Afraid this did not insure him against harm, he took boxing lessons. At the hour of crisis he was ready. The office bully, not suspecting what he was letting himself in for, grabbed Wright's hat and threw it down the stairs. Quick as a flash Wright swung at him. The blow broke his foe's glasses and sent him flying off his stool. The man rushed him, savagely waving a knife seized from a handy table. He slashed Wright until the blood dripped down into his shoes. Wright knocked him out with a drawing tool. Was Wright at fault in any way in provoking the attack? He could be an exasperating person—at least in his later years. He had the same arrogance and unlimited self-esteem as had Adler. Perhaps he was a brash youth. But if his fellow employees still disliked him, the fight taught them not to tangle with him.

To enter upon a social life, he placed himself in the care of his mother's brother, the Reverend Doctor Lloyd-Jones.

At a dance under the minister's patronage, he met the girl he wanted for his wife, Catherine Tobin. Both families disapproved. But he had no ear for critics, and the marriage took place. Professionally he was driving ahead fast. As a sign of the high regard of Adler & Sullivan for him, the firm bound him with a five-year contract. It also gave him land in a Chicago suburb, Oak Park. There was room on it for two houses. His mother moved into the small one already there. He designed the other for himself and his bride.

Now the spendthrift in Wright took over. He would always wear a mink collar he could not always afford. Unwilling to wait for the uncertain morrow to enjoy a handsome home, he made purchases rashly. His table was set with expensive silver, his vases filled with flowers, his floors covered with thick rugs. A grocer hounded him for an $850 bill until he borrowed the money to pay it. Expenditures usually kept an imprudent distance ahead of income. He still invited friends to elegant dinners beyond his means. He would not stop dressing his wife and several children in fine clothes and escorting them to concerts in his revered Sullivan's Auditorium.

In time to come, he advised young men not to follow his profession in the hope of getting rich. He himself spent several fortunes and lived in style. Some architects, like Sullivan, Richardson, and Burnham, as well as Wright, suffered from a wide ostentatious streak. They worked for the wealthy. To look wealthy might help secure commissions. Perhaps they had to appear to be keeping up with the Joneses in order to get the Joneses' business. They loved to live like the Joneses anyway.

We ought not to blame Wright since, when he got what he wanted, we did, too: more of his handiwork. Debts chained him overtime to his drawing board. One extra job was the James Charnley house in Chicago. Red brick on a stone foundation, it is three stories high. This is a carefully balanced structure, with the bulk distributed evenly. The sharp, regular profile suggests it is an arrangement of oversize Fröbel blocks.

Wright's last big task with Adler & Sullivan was the Transportation Building at the Columbian Exposition in Chicago. In 1893, Sullivan discovered his cocky young assistant was secretly catering to clients of his own. Feeling betrayed and perhaps cheated, he hauled him on the carpet and ordered him to stop. Wright might have been placated, but the infuriated Sullivan's rebuke infuriated Wright. He stamped out for good. He admitted the break was his fault. The admission came only years later, however, when again he referred to Sullivan as "beloved master." Despite the injured egos, Wright was probably better off alone. The world was better off, too, since the separation freed him to chart his own creative path.

Though Wright, like Sullivan, condemned the Columbian Exposition of 1893 in Chicago as a staggering setback to his profession, it may have exerted an unexpected, indirect influence on him. He could dismiss Georgian and Renaissance, mission and Colonial styles as irrelevant and useless. Yet he might have learned unconsciously, since he has denied it, from a small reproduction of a Japanese wood temple erected on the Chicago grounds. It revealed its elementary post-and-lintel construction quite frankly. The roof stretched far down over the wall. The white plaster contrasted freshly with the black timbers. It was simple, compact, and intimate with the outdoors. Wright advocated this sort of merger. He would crusade for broken barriers, the elimination of walls, the intermingling of outside and inside.

Numerous temple features are incorporated in his Prairie House, so-called, probably his greatest gift to us.

In 1893, Wright set up his office in the heart of the Windy City, Chicago. Extra work space had to be rented near his new home. The moves resulted in more mortgages, more bills, more busyness, and happily more buildings. His expert staff included the first woman licensed to practice architecture in Illinois.

He now loomed up as a character with some public recognition. The country boy who climbed from poverty to wealth, from obscurity to fame, and who licked the bully looked a lot like a Horatio Alger hero. His early successes with Sullivan and his nervy, ill-tempered separation were grist to the gossip monger. A real-estate developer felt such confidence in his spectacular promise that he offered to pay for four years of Rome and Paris for Wright and his family. Wright decided against it.

A lawyer with a wealthy clientele asked for a home. He had in mind something conventional, embellished, however, by Wright's renown. "Hanged if I'll take a back street to the morning train to avoid being laughed at. I want it black and white—half-timbered—the Tudor sort of thing," he said. Such a professional had the habit of giving orders. Wright, no less a professional, did not have the habit of obeying. He needed the money, however, and he accepted the commission. He asserted later that no client "must" take a job he does not like. Concomitantly, no architect must build anything he does not like. This was a noble principle, noble even though it did not cost him a cent's worth of business. Usually an architect has only sympathetic clients. Usually a man who wants a house approaches only the expert whose stuff he knows and favors. Each expects to get what he wants even before a word is spoken. It is a circle, the opposite of a vicious one.

But there are troubles. Most people must borrow for a home. Bankers are conservative and insist on their money back. They know the styles that are salable. They are not crusading for any new look. Of course the builder has a perfect right to suit his taste. But suppose he commits himself to something extreme, which might be criticized as a freak? Suppose he runs out of funds and foreclosure is necessary? Ten times more buyers show up for the "safe" and conventional structure than for the modern, fresh, and different. For years banks would not risk a penny on anything out of the ordinary rut. They liked architects, even avant-garde architects, but they loved a sure investment.

Other persons are involved in the chain process. Every step might be a stumbling block. The mill owner balks at doing jobs for the way-out architect. The decorator shies away from the modernist—who usually prefers doing without him, for he has his own ideas about inside as well as outside.

Other hurdles to discourage the investor would be laughable if they did not seriously affect the innovator. Men hate to sign up for a building that might be made fun of. This particular lawyer wanted a home, not a place requiring his vigilant defense against all sorts of jibes. Might not even his friends question his taste and judgment if he lived in such a home? Could a fellow who believed in such "crazy" things really be a dependable lawyer, doctor, broker, insurance agent, or manufacturer?

Strangers, too, interfered. Wright fans in later years acted as if any Wright house, instead of being private, was a public museum. They practically demanded admittance; how does an owner dare be stingy with such a treasure! Harassed owners hired watch dogs, fenced their property in, even changed the name on the mail box to fool the fanatics.

Another Wright house dating from the James Charnley period is the William H. Winslow one in the Chicago suburb of River Forest. Here, too, the familiar decorations, the extras, the superficialities were eliminated. In contrast to the vertical skyscraper, the horizontal is stressed. Even the fact that it is only two stories high increases the emphasis on the side-to-side stretch. The lines of the roof, with its long overhang, reach far and unbroken. The tops of the urns in front are flattened. There is again a Richardsonian heaviness particularly about the chimney and a corner stair tower. Wright tried a trick that became a favorite of his: in order to save a large tree standing where he had planned a wall and roof, he left a hole in the overhang so it could continue growing. There is one drawback: when the tree dies, no other can be trained in its place.

While with Sullivan, the eager Wright picked up a smattering of information about *Art Nouveau* and William Morris. He had the opportunity to judge the effectiveness of Sullivan's ornament. Wright designed clothes for his wife Catherine. Like Morris and Richardson, he occasionally made furniture. Though he improved on the commercial mass-produced article, it was not completely satisfactory. He preferred abstract excellence to comfort. A chair's function was to beautify a room primarily and secondarily to afford a restful and easy seat. Most architects would agree. Some, though they would not say so, might feel that the best thing about making a chair or table was the fun of twisting and shaping steel, aluminum, plywood, or plastic—and let somebody else sit in it. Wright's high-backed dining-room chair was smart. But it was more architecture than furniture. To occupy it during dinner was a privilege but not necessarily a pleasure. His chairs and tables were of course intended for his own buildings. An occasional contract specified that he would design the inside as well as the out. In comparison with Richardson, he charged six to eight percent of total cost as his fee, but for a wealthy client he upped it to fifteen percent. One of his complex constructions tagged as a chair is exhibited in the Museum of Modern Art in New York. If, as is said, he confessed he was not the best furniture designer alive, it was a true confession and perhaps a unique one. The chances are he did not believe a word of it.

He was a fast worker. Sullivan sketched the Wainwright Building in three minutes, he told Wright. In this, Wright imitated him.

Another early work of Wright's in Oak Park was Unity Temple, opened for worship in 1908. Wright proudly identified it as "the first concrete monolith to come from the forms as architecture completely finished." There were other concrete buildings, among them Auguste Perret's epochal apartments in the Rue Franklin in Paris. But this church was Wright's first conscious demonstration of his personal method. It was organic architecture. By his description and practice, this is a style that does not strain for effect, does not copy, employs materials as they themselves dictate, regardless of fashion. Gothic was organic, he explained. It is less building than growing, as recommended by Sullivan. What was more, in Wright's peculiar and unique view, it grew not only out of its components and function but also out of its environment. Unity Temple was conceived as an integral part of the street and community, as other structures were parts of a hill or woods.

The designer clung to the theory that a building should reveal its purpose throughout. We would need several guesses before deciding this was a church. Wright himself, when asked, could explain only haltingly how the envelope fitted the content. Since it was all of a piece, it expressed the Christian unity of the Divine and the human. The auditorium, which the congregation entered along ramps from the pulpit side, had the shape of a Greek cross. The gracious and roomy interior might be considered a symbol of the religious spirit. The outside was a large gray pile of concrete-with-pebbles intentionally left rough. Temple authorities, a little worried about the reaction of staid parishioners, issued a statement that emphasized accurately "the quiet surfaces, unbroken lines, and restful interiors, shielded from the noise of Lake Street." One thing surely to be worshiped in it was Wright's genius for innovation.

Another temple important to him was the Japanese exhibit at the Columbian Exposition in Chicago. He did not forget. Among other reminders of the oriental island included in it were remarkable prints. For years Japanese prints had impressed European painters, as their art clearly showed. Some canny Americans were buying them. These matters among others sent Wright to Japan in 1905. The country fascinated him. In appearance he turned native and wore Japanese robes to visit shops for the prints that were the foundation of his own collection—the collection he would sell, as Sullivan did, in hard times.

Just before hard times caught up with him, he produced the Frederick Carleton Robie House. He had plenty of money for this—he no more enjoyed skimping for clients than for himself. Robie allocated $14,000 for the lot, $35,-000 for the building proper, and $10,000 for furniture Wright would design or select. The result was hailed by the *Architectural Record* as "one of the seven most notable residences ever built in America." In the opinion of Peter Blake, the architectural critic, it may "be considered the most influential house of its era."

Erected near the University of Chicago campus, it has narrowly escaped the destruction that befell Wright's earlier Larkin Building in Buffalo, New York. After that was sold for scrap, the site was cleared for parking. When Robie had finished with his house, it passed through the hands of a second private owner into the possession of the Chicago Theological Seminary. It was a valuable property and lot. The Seminary could use the money. Wright's friend, the poet Carl Sandburg, rightly said its loss would be "irretrievable." The loss was averted when contractor William Zeckendorf bought it for offices.

The most satisfactory way to view it today is perhaps in the model in the Museum of Modern Art in New York. According to rumor, Robie hoped it would look like a steamship. If he did not get anything with a seaworthy air, neither did he get anything traditional. It had the substantiality, the sturdy appearance of impregnability that we associate with Richardson's thick-bodied structures. Though it is three stories tall, it consists chiefly of two working floors. With the basement eliminated and the entire structure resting flat on the surface of the ground, the top two floors are the utility areas. The essential fixed features are bunched in the middle: sinks, heating system, power lines, plumbing. Except for these, you may look clear through from front to back with no more than a dooknob to block the view—just as the sight line in the modern theater is unbroken. Visually the whole thing is open.

Yet note how importantly it differs from the Crystal Palace, which also was open. As the Robie House has glass walls, so did the Crystal Palace. Paxton's walls separated the inside from the outside. Wright's let the two merge. Paxton's are walls; Wright's are glass. Here is the almost measureless distance between two eras, two ages. As Wright said, "The outside gradually came in more and more and the inside went outside more." It sounds like a phrase out of Gertrude Stein.

Take a squint at the model and you reduce it to several horizontal edges, like the fronts of shelves. This characteristic of Wright's stands out more plainly in a house we shall visit later, Fallingwater.

His goal was simplicity. He discarded two common areas: the "unwholesome" basement and the attic with the bulging dormer that ruined the clean roof line he favored. There are two squat chimneys; later he preferred one. A house in his opinion should consist of the fewest possible parts—some fifty thousand pieces go into the average dwelling. One aim was to abolish "the room as a box and the house as another box." To accomplish this, he slimmed walls down in effect into screens, much as bricks had developed into curtains. The box to his mind was a Fascist symbol—to the Russians the cube just as arbitrarily represented purity. If his notion guided him to more open and flexible space, we welcome the achievement and ignore the reason. An architect's words, like a painter's, rarely speak so dependably as his works.

The Frederick Carleton Robie House is the famous Prairie House. It contained an early incorporated garage. It had a big fireplace. Cellar and attic disappeared. There were ribbon windows—that is, they ran together horizontally. They also ran right around corners with no posts to mark the angle. The roof's deep overhang protected the walls and glass and kept out glaring sun. The entire house rested on a concrete slab in which heat pipes were imbedded.

If this is not machine-made, it at least looked it. Ruskin's unreasoning hatred of the machine had yielded to a reasoning acceptance. The modernist turns to it at every chance. Why do by hand what can be done mechanically? Why produce a unique object when it can be infinitely and perfectly duplicated? Hence the painter, aware that only one person can possess his canvas, is thankful for the multiple silk-screen process. Hence, in part, the popularity of the camera with countless copies of its pictures possible and the moving picture, which reproduces a play over and over. The Europeans were just like us. They wanted to build houses with a difference out of parts that were insofar as possible without a difference. Standardized bricks, shingles, and clapboards were familiar. All of a sudden it was magically possible to standardize many other parts: panes of glass, window frames, doors, steel beams, concrete sections, cement blocks, fixtures of all sorts. The apparent advance made by the Robie House in the direction of standardization fascinated students and scholars abroad. They also admired its rectangular forms and orderly design suggestive of Cubism. This was a painting style already copied by architects in other countries. It could have struck Wright as another way to play with Fröbel blocks. Only a year or two after the Robie success, an illustrated account of Wright's work was published in Germany. It affected Europeans profoundly. Later it bounded back and affected Americans.

Thanks to his daring, his inventiveness, and his originality, Wright at forty was famous. For a miserable decade, personal problems interfered disastrously with his career. A man so intense, vital, and self-confident at his office tends to carry the independence and arrogance over into private affairs. As he brooked no nay-sayers on his staff, he brooked none either in his home. If he was free to build as no one else ever had, was he not free to behave as no one else? He had a large family and the wife he had embraced impetuously in his youth. Somehow this did not satisfy a man greedy for the fullest and broadest experiences. Disappointment broke out in fits of temper. He felt worn out. A commission went wrong, though with so many others going wonderfully right, it should not have mattered. After the pattern set by his father, he walked out of his home. He eloped to Europe with a client's wife.

When his mother turned over to him the family's two hundred acres in Wisconsin, he planned there his Taliesin, a studio, home, refuge, and fortress, named after a Welsh bard, Taliesin, meaning "Shining Brow." Wright sited it on a slope and raised his walls out of local stone. It was one of his great achievements, or on the way to being that, for he kept changing and enlarging—and never finishing. A tragedy of such unmitigated and absolute horror occurred there that it shared the stark quality of Greek drama. An employee went berserk and killed seven people. His victims were the woman with whom Wright had eloped to Europe, her young son and daughter, the son of a carpenter, and three other employees. The madman was found hiding in the boiler and died of poison at once, before any trial.

To an unknown woman who wrote a letter of sympathy, Wright answered with an invitation to visit him. She became his nagging, suspicious second wife, who hurt him as much as if she were his enemy. She became that in the end. The genius, who would not let anyone tell him how to build, would not let anyone tell him how to manage his personal life. His conduct was publicly condemned. Fellow architects ignored him. Business fell off ruinously. At one time he had signed a commission every couple of months. Now for a decade his estimated income may have sunk as low as $2,000 a year. This was a wretched comedown for a man in the habit of pocketing generous fees and living in luxury.

Misfortune could not repress him. He invited some colleagues to a restaurant only to find he did not have enough cash to pay the bill. They paid for their own dinners. Bill collectors would not be fobbed off. The sheriff sent an officer to lock up the studio and seal it for a $1,500 debt. Wright won again; granted half an hour's leeway, he hustled out and borrowed $10,000. With the $1,500 obligation settled, the rest was squandered in a mad spree on an overcoat, art objects, furniture, and a pair of grand pianos.

As a taskmaster he was less aloof than Sullivan; yet he had a touchy and capricious streak. Relations with underlings were usually cordial. They enjoyed advantages denied by other firms, he claimed. They met clients; their advice was asked and heeded; certain responsibilities were assigned them. But he kept a close check on every operation and had the last word. The main structural elements and all minor details required his O.K. He was the boss. He was even a jealous boss. He quarreled meanly with a sculptor whose work he tried to take credit for. Later, Wright publicly admitted that a statement of his had created the wrong impression. He made sure it would never happen again. From then on his buildings got along with little or no sculpture.

In his entire career, no assignment resulted in so many headlines as his Imperial Hotel in Tokyo. A New York art dealer, acquainted with him as a print connoisseur, introduced him to financiers backing the project. Assuming their ideas would be conventional, Wright doubted they would award him the contract. His plans, with their decided Western basis and yet Oriental and exotic flavor, won them over. In 1916, he and his second wife crossed the Pacific. In his own mind, he would help Japan to change from wood to concrete. It was his aim also, he has stated with the pretentiousness that irks some people, to help lift her "from her knees to her feet." Finally, thanks to him, the Japanese would learn how to guard against their devastating earthquakes.

His problem was a hotel on a three-hundred by five-hundred-foot site. This huge structure would be put together so that a major temblor would not take it apart. Viewed in a vertical section, that is, a slice down through the ground, his plot, as he described it, was "composed of sixty feet of liquid mud overlaid by eight feet of filled soil. The filling was about the consistency of hard cheese." This presented an apparently impossible challenge. Yet Wright remembered his experiences in Chicago with a similar underpinning, or lack of one. What worked in America ought to work in Japan. He also hit on another idea: let the mud help instead of hinder. Why not treat it as a cushion against quakes? His hotel would ride the semiliquid, "float . . . somewhat as a battleship floats on salt water." By his theory, the hotel, instead of fighting the temblor, should go with it—the boxer had not forgotten how to roll with the punch. The earth shocks would wash harmlessly around the anchorage.

Wood piles eight feet long were hammered down into the earth, or the "hard cheese." The woman laborers sang as they pulled rhythmically on the ropes of the pile drivers. When the piles were withdrawn, the holes they left, about two feet apart, were plugged with concrete. Atop these pins, carefully leveled off, Wright balanced his great structure. This foundation was a lot cheaper than the solid base regularly in use in Tokyo—total costs, however, much exceeded Wright's estimate. Everything was fireproof except window frames and sashes, which would have been too expensive in metal. The bulk of the hotel was assembled in sixty-foot sections. Larger masses of reinforced concrete would theoretically crack at Tokyo temperatures.

"To insure stability I carried the floor and roof loads as a waiter carries his tray on his upraised arm and fingers," Wright explained. The friction of the hotel's weight glued it in place. Oya, a stone resembling limestone, was quite light and common. The islanders complained it was not only common but also cheap. But the American liked it, had his way, and bought an entire quarry. The walls of the hotel were oya, thin brick and reinforced concrete. Light copper tiles covered the roof. A huge reflecting pool lay picturesquely near the entrance.

Besides technical headaches, there were domestic squabbles. His unhappy wife badgered him constantly. While he should have been wrestling with professional matters, she diverted his attention with petty personal affairs. American architects passing through Tokyo gratuitously criticized Wright's design and construction. Other Americans objected to his love for the Japanese. Some doubts bothered the Japanese, and the government refused a construction permit. But one Japanese sponsor, unshaken in his confidence, became Wright's guarantor, and there was no official interference. The hotel was finally in operation in July, 1922.

Just thirteen ominous months later while Wright was in Los Angeles, newsboys raced through the streets crying "Extra!" Catastrophe had struck. A "terrific temblor" had wiped out Tokyo and Yokohama. Descriptions of the disaster, though they were vague, kept pouring in. Soon a newspaper, sure it had a story to take the cocky Wright down a peg, phoned that his Imperial Hotel was a total loss. Wright laughed. He warned his informer indignantly that if the yarn was published, it would have to be retracted.

Would he have dared bet on it? He was even more worried when the accusing paper—as cocksure as Wright had ever been—ran the story on page one. Could the worst have

happened? He had experimented with a method still untested. Perhaps he had been wrong. He would not be the
first, but he would hate to be convicted—to be found wrong
on the front pages in many cities, wrong among rivals who
would gloat over his error, wrong in his own chosen life
work.

There was a long and harrowing week. Contradictory re-
ports tormented him day after day. At last a cable arrived:
"Hotel stands undamaged as monument of your genius.
Hundreds of homeless provided for by perfectly maintained
service. Congratulations." It was signed by Wright's own
constant defender on the finance board. Even the reflecting
pool had helped: The water put out fires in the woodwork.
The posts that cushioned each sixty-foot section had enabled
it to resist the fury of the quake. The press that had mocked
him retracted its charges. It is, however, true that the hotel
was not the only sizable structure to survive. Quakes are capricious. But the American's theory had been corroborated.
More buildings would have ridden out the temblor if they
had floated on a cushion like his.

The unsavory machinations of the woman impulsively invited into his life as his wife were climaxed with a night he
had to spend in jail in Minneapolis. His reputation was entitled to a boost to compensate for a series of nasty blows he
had sustained. Friends rallied to his support. The personal
slander, they protested, should not go so far as to inflict
professional injury. After fires damaged Taliesin, Wright incorporated his home, house, and school, where loyalty to the
leader was never shaken in the least. A mechanical device
produced some unexpected and welcome revenue. He married another time, the last time, and for good—for his good,
too. An obscure college, Florida Southern College, was short
on money but long on ideas. Would he design its campus

with only the prospect of uncertain future recompense? In the end, his commission may have totaled $100,000.

As the dire influence of the depression of 1929 started to wane and business perked up again, Wright had the chance at a major commercial project. It was the Research Tower and Administration Building for S. C. Johnson & Son in Racine, Wisconsin. The floors in the tower cantilevered from a central steel mast or core. The same skeleton would be the spine for his more elaborate and decorative Price Tower in Bartlesville, Oklahoma.

The Administration Building caught the public fancy. The roof over the principal open space, a workroom, rested on a cluster of twenty-four-foot-tall columns. Famous now, their flattened tops and slender shafts resembled giant lily pads. The calculated load per shaft was six tons. Know-it-all officialdom maintained such a burden would crush them. Wright staged a test for all the world to see and marvel at. His name and the controversy drew a crowd to the demonstration. Police raised barricades to help keep control of the situation. Endowed with the knack for showmanship shared by many artists, Wright was the ringmaster. At his signals, a crane dropped ton after ton of scrap metal on the platform atop his lily pad. Only after sixty tons were piled on did the fragile-looking column collapse. This proved a factor of safety, so-called, of almost ten to one. Four to one made it legal and acceptable. Officials' doubts were dispelled. Wright was in a transport of joy at confounding his critics. The Johnson company got a lot of first-rate publicity free. All new buildings have an advertising value. This had much more than its share, thanks to the radical design and the near-skyscraper proportions and the Wright circus. In the first two days after it was opened to the public, thirty thousand people visited it, and thousands have gone since.

Wright himself could be caustic about other people's work. Finis Farr, in his biography, collected a few comments: the Metropolitan Museum in New York was a "Protestant barn"; Rockefeller Center was "the crime of crimes against humanity"; the United Nations Secretariat "a gravestone"; the Seagram Building for the distillers "a whiskey bottle on a card table." Years before Wright had, curiously, envisioned as a handsome possibility a structure all glass and bronze, a description that fits the Seagram Building.

Countering these are some damaging complaints about Wright's own Guggenheim Museum. Its purpose was the display of abstract art. It also, in its opening days and weeks and months, attracted more people for a view of the novel container than for the novel content. Architectural critic Peter Blake, as biting as Wright, credited the Guggenheim Foundation with having a "fabulous" architectural gem. He hailed Wright's only completely successful plastic, fluid, continuous work. Then he suggested slyly, now was the time for the foundation to put up a building where it could show the paintings.

The museum, which looms up challengingly on upper Fifth Avenue overlooking Central Park, is a spiral. Wright had already experimented with this form. For Pittsburgh, he proposed a spiral garage. Inside a small store in San Francisco, he arranged an attractive ramp curving from ground level to mezzanine. His only other work in New York City, the Mercedes-Benz showroom, is also a short sharp ramp for displaying autos. The idea of a continuous display space had intrigued other architects. Their purpose was to break away from the traditional static arrangement of rows or clusters of boxlike halls. Le Corbusier devised an ingenious square spiral. A long corridor kept bending at a right angle at the corners. All on ground level, it could be indefinitely expanded. Perhaps the Guggenheim, too, could be enlarged by running the spiral up above its present six-story height.

It is an upside-down ziggurat. The visitor rides the elevator to the top and follows the one-lane gallery the easy way downward and back to the central court. Though other innovations of Wright's are criticized, this was good enough to copy. Edward Durrell Stone's still newer Gallery of Modern Art on Columbus Circle in New York City also starts the regular tour at the top and bids the art lover good-by at the exit at the bottom.

Wright's troubles began with the city, which delayed its approval of his extraordinary plans for the Guggenheim for two years—with material costs slowly rising all the time. Once his museum was erected, it was attacked by art authorities. They, or some of them, charged him with outright indifference to painting. His only interest, they complained, was to play with an architectural idea. It was just too bad if the picture viewer was not wisely served meanwhile. They rightly pointed out that Wright's original plans—later modified to be sure—did not admit enough light to the principal display space, the outside wall, that is, the wall with outdoors and daylight behind it. Further, they feel uncomfortable standing on the slope. It is slight, but the stance is not natural. It obliges them to think of their balance when they prefer to think of an oil painting or a sculpture. They enjoy, it is true, the splendid vertical opening in general; taken as a whole, this gives the sensation of a vast hall while retaining some of the privacy of separate chambers.

A legitimate gripe understandable by laymen as well as experts concerns the continuous inner rail of the ramp. The inside edge has been turned up as a piecrust is turned up at the rim. The comparison is too pat. As the crust is turned up only a bit, so comparatively is the concrete. A visitor peering over may suffer a dizzy spell. Many visitors cautiously set themselves firmly on their heels before they lean too near that edge. Are they afraid it will give way? It will not. Could they fall over? Some of them think so. It does not seem to be a safe guard rail. Why wasn't it higher? Perhaps Wright worried about cutting off some badly needed light. Or he may have believed he might mar the design of his interior. Worst of all, it might impose on this ribbonlike one-way gallery precisely the boxed-in effect he proposed to eliminate.

If the Guggenheim is the most talked-of museum, the most talked-of house is Fallingwater. In the 1930's Edgar Kaufmann, Jr., one of Wright's pupils at Taliesin, persuaded his father to hire Wright for a family project. The elder Kaufmann was a Pittsburgh department-store magnate. He and his wife spent summer weekends beside Bear Run, a tributary of the Youghiogheny River. It was isolated, wild, and picturesque, and they loved it. They took a particular delight in resting on a great boulder above the stream and listening to the waterfall. They longed for a house there. Wright had a quick and practiced eye for assessing the potentialities of a site. On a one-day visit, he tramped over the place from the river bed up the banks on both sides. Three weeks later he submitted his plan. Young Kaufmann offered a few suggestions and Mrs. Kaufmann a bit of advice. Otherwise, the house conformed to the original design.

Presented to the public in 1963 and opened formally in 1964, this fascinating structure attracted nearly twenty thousand visitors its first season. Crowds kept coming, although the nearest big city is Pittsburgh, seventy miles away. The building hangs or rides on a steep slope. A flood once lifted the rushing water almost to the first floor and pounded the place till it shook. The only damage was to some sculpture swept off low pedestals around the grounds.

Trees surround the house and hide it. They are not small and young, either, but have achieved a grand towering growth. Like any worthy architect, Wright was happy to spare them. Furthermore, he used them lovingly, working them into his vision of the place. It could be called Green Oaks or the Beeches as well as Fallingwater. Bear Run tumbling over the stepped rocks causes a constant dull roar. Today wide lawns line the main approach. On the original several hundred acres, there was no grass to mow. The grounds remained untouched and in the wild state or were planted with high, thick masses of rhododendron. The first view of the house comes from a bridge a little below house level. Anchored to concrete bases like gigantic brackets, three floors, or tables, reach out over the water. Exactly as in the Robie House, these areas are open except at the utility core in the middle. Again this is like looking through empty bookcase shelves.

The inexperienced local contractor reportedly ran into trouble. His concrete at first was poured on boards improperly prepared, so that it stuck, and next on boards without waterproofing, so that they leaked. A common charge leveled at Wright's houses is that they spring a leak. One exasperated owner telephoned to complain the water was dripping on a guest in his chair. Wright supposedly answered: "Then move the chair away."

A guide recalls another anecdote about the contractor. In accordance with specifications, the platforms were projected overhead dizzily. When he had to knock out the props, he was afraid tons of concrete would tumble down on his head. He refused to take the responsibility. Wright was summoned. He climbed down to the bottom level right into the death trap, as the contractor had feared it might be. He was as confident—and with good reason—as he had been in dropping sixty tons of scrap on his lily pad in Racine. The supports were removed. According to medieval custom, Wright, the master builder, was first to risk his neck on his finished work. Fallingwater still stands. It looks as everlasting as the rock to which it is clamped. Perhaps the contractor could justify his timidity in part by pointing to the doubting Thomases on the town building commission. They had refused to approve Wright's original plans. The defiant architect imbedded their official condemnation somewhere in his concrete. He expected it would not be recovered this side of doomsday.

The best part of the house is the view of it: daring, majestic, serene, beautifully harmonizing with the woodland setting. This cannot be, one feels, any more than a castle in fairyland can be. Yet this is splendidly before us. Next best are the views from inside. On the first floor or terrace are the living room and dining room. From this recessed area, we see a slice of the growth of trees on the opposite bank. Neither the tops nor bottoms show. A knowing cameraman might trim his print in this shorthand fashion.

Ribbon windows are set far inside the outer edges of the decks. They stretch around on three sides and have no corners, that favorite Wright arrangement. The eye is not obliged to differentiate between a factitious right and left where, in fact, a single landscape expands before it. The flooring is slabs of local stone left raw outdoors but waxed within the glass walls. Dining-room chairs have only three legs, so that they do not teeter on this uneven surface. To the traditional huge Wright fireplace, a sentimental touch has been added. Running out shallowly in front of it, breaking irregularly through the floor, lie two flat fingers of the boulder on which the Kaufmanns had loved to sit. The chimney, the fireplace, and the compact kitchen, with heavy equipment, help to anchor the building on the slope. They balance the weight cantilevered dramatically above the cascading water.

Up a curving walk at the back stands the guest house. The cement-slab canopy above the passageway is supported by posts on only one side, the outside; it slopes up slightly on the inside. This shape gives it its staying power, for the sharper the pull of gravity, the more the arch is compressed on itself and reinforced. Some stairs in the main house lead down from the first floor to the water's edge. Yet they really lead nowhere, neither to a swimming pool nor to a waiting boat, and we can only climb back up again. A comparable path beside the guest house guides us to steps that drop down toward the woods. They, too, stop right there. It is a surrealist feature, yet not to Wright's mind; for him, both flights act, in part, to integrate the structures in their setting. They look and behave as though they belonged there, or were hooked there, and merge with the surroundings. We find ourselves wondering whether the brush and woods were there before the houses or perhaps the houses before the brush and woods. In an inside corridor, there is natural running water. A stream leaked regularly from the hillside—a leak the occupant enjoyed and Wright intentionally permitted. Instead of damming it up, he dug a narrow channel, let it trickle prettily along the corridor, and piped it below out of sight and outdoors.

One tree grows through a contrived opening among the beams above the driveway. The garage is a carport with a wide roof. The concrete is pale apricot or tan. The Venetian red of the metal window frames matches the borders of the shield-shaped lights sunk in outdoor walls and ceilings. The furniture is mostly made or chosen by Wright. Ingenious stools manage to be both firm and soft. A long, low flat bench runs beside the principal window. Cushions are padded with foam rubber reportedly for the first time. The terrace floors conceal a ventilating space, and the heat is radiant, though there are a few surface outlets. For low tables, there are heavy tree-trunk segments; for rugs, the furs of raccoon, fox, skunk, and other local animals. The very walls consist of miniatures of the house as a whole. Flat, thin slabs of stone project from the concrete bed in uneven layers like so many small shelves.

Lamps are oblong metal tubes cut away on two sides and focused either the long way or endwise. There is a patently makeshift arrangement beside two built-in desks: the inner corners had to be gouged out for tall narrow ventilating doors to swing open. Wright was not a practical man and did not approve of screens. Mrs. Kaufmann, who must have been driven off that exposed boulder many a summer evening by mosquitoes, had them installed. Wright was impractical in other respects—though it must be remembered that Fallingwater was not intended for year-round occupancy. Ceilings are low and rooms tend to be dark. The four bedrooms are uncomfortably small. The corridors are very narrow. At the head of interior flights of stairs, a foot-high guard rail is, in effect, no guard at all. Outside, this hazard is worse. The concrete-floor shelves run out far from the hill-side mooring, and then their edges turn up like the inner side of the Guggenheim ramp. But here the wall or railing is lower and the danger greater. The Kaufmanns had no children to worry about when this was built. But a grownup could topple over a railing below his center of gravity. Timid or sensible visitors warned by the roar of water way below are extremely wary about looking over.

If the water sometimes sounds loud, the noise can be shut out by tight-fitting doors. However, it seems certain the house is damp. One admission of it, and a minor counter to it, is the woven cane used instead of solid wood in the trays in clothes closets to permit free circulation of air.

One basic trouble lies in what we define as the module or Modulor. This is a unit of measurement, and a highly personal one, one length for one man, another for another, depending on caprice, chance, and a variety of things. Mies van der Rohe has his unit; Le Corbusier his, called the Modulor; and Wright his. Wright's was five feet eight and a half inches, his own height, plus his raised arm. He theorized that the bedroom ceiling should be just high enough above the floor so that he, standing, could lift his arm and place the flat of his hand on it. Wrightian architecture, as he admitted, might have had a different look if architect Wright had been taller or shorter—and, we add, less egotistical. He built his house not to the measure of the Kaufmanns, but himself, the man who would not inhabit it.

Yet this measure, alien to us, is nevertheless an aspect of the intimate, personal flavor we admire in Wright's work. We cannot say his house is beautiful because he is five feet eight and a half inches tall; nor can we say this measure has no connection with the undeniable beauty. He believed in the measure; the beauty is there; some mysterious bond unites them. The tall visitor may bear witness to it for us. He runs a double risk. Because of his height, he is more apt to tumble over into the water and, for the same reason, he is surer of cracking his head on the ceiling. He still salutes Wright as the incomparable master. With even more faults, the house would still be a wonder and a marvel because through and through it is Frank Lloyd Wright—Wright and his flair, his taste, his adventurousness, his eye, his mind, his imagination, and his five feet eight and a half inches.

Wright created for romantic reasons: to fit the setting, to

please the eye. We do not in the long run assess a house only by its convenience and practicality. Glamor importantly affects our judgment. Life in a palace or castle, unhandy and uncomfortable though it might be, offers benefits denied by the ordinary humdrum house. If Fallingwater is not adjusted to the average person and his wants, still the chance to live there would be one of the grand adventures of our time, one of the memorable experiences.

We shall meet other architects who define a dwelling in terms of traffic, working, eating, sleeping, and so on. Le Corbusier called the proper house a machine to live in. Wright agrees: yes, a house is a machine, but it begins to be architecture only after the machine business is disposed of. If the dimensions or some other aspect displease us, Wright might bluntly tell us to move our chair away. The wonder remains.

The great buildings of the past, he noted, partook of the character of monuments. It seemed as if a sculptor shaped the outside and someone else hollowed it out for human use. Wright with his knack for the dramatic, as every design shows, liked the outside to impose. But while he was not so-cial-minded like Le Corbusier, he was more practical than his old-fashioned predecessors. He never neglected the fundamental requirements of a dwelling. He could have paid more heed to the requirements of the dweller.

We thank him partly or wholly for foam-rubber seats, indirect lighting, radiant heat, ribbon windows, the clean line, the simplified form, the harmonious setting, and a host of other improvements in homes and offices. Most of all, he left us an image of the independent, daring adventurer in the basic art. If he did not always build perfectly, he was always the perfect builder.

For what he gave us, we gave to him embarrassingly little

—something like a couple of gold medals. His contacts were incredibly broad, his range of interests extraordinary. He began in poverty and ended in riches. He made the most distinguished friends and the most distinguished enemies. He pretended with superb arrogance there was only one valid height for a man. Out of the contradictions, extremes, and unreasonablenesses came a more beautiful America and the splendid prospect of an America more beautiful still.

11 | Le Corbusier

If we enjoyed our two walks at the start of this story, let's try a third. This is a real one that took place shortly before World War II. It was mostly a ride, though, for it covered quite a few miles. The place was Paris, and the goal a house in the suburb of Garches. I was the one to make the trip. In Garches, two Americans, Michael Stein and his wife, lived in a large house built for them by the Frenchman Le Corbusier. It was one of the sights of the day. Despite some remodeling, it still is. Michael Stein collected the paintings of Henri Matisse. He was the brother of the famous collector and writer Gertrude Stein.

At first, I walked from my hotel along the Seine River

near the Louvre Museum. From the Gardens of the Tuile-
ries, I crossed the vast Place de la Concorde with its fountains
and statues. I followed the wide Champs-Elysées, a grand
boulevard not so cluttered then with salesrooms and not so
dazzling with neon. Near its end, almost in the shadow of the
Arc de Triomphe rising in its star-shaped square, Michael
Stein met me in his car. He drove through the Bois de Boulogne, or Boulogne Woods. One of the continent's most
beautiful parks, its shaded roads wind around pretty ponds.
Across the Seine, the auto climbed and bounced over
cobblestones through a quaint square. Then we passed
through the Park of St. Cloud, where French kings once
reigned from a château now destroyed. At last, on a hilltop,
we pulled off the road and there we were.

The house occupied a narrow lot. Since neighbors might
some day move in close, the two sides were blank areas, mere
service walls to the architect and of only practical use to the
inhabitants. An enormous tilted concrete canopy stretched
out like a plane wing above the door toward the street. A
pair of ribbon windows ran from edge to edge of the
street side. The true front was the back. From the car we
looked right through the house to the yard in back with its
winding walks. The house proper began, in effect, a floor
above Wright's Prairie House. That, in turn, began a floor
above the traditional house. Wright eliminated the cellar and
Le Corbusier eliminated the first floor, putting it where our
second is.

Perhaps we should reconsider our method of numbering.
The French describe the ground floor as "level with the
roadway." Their first floor is our second. A handsome skyscraper in New York devotes its ground floor to nothing more
than reception desk and elevators. A Mies van der Rohe res-
idence abroad was entered from the top floor on the street

with the other floor dropping away on a slope to the rear. Who can say which is number one? Occasionally we enter through the basement. In a huge complex like Rockefeller Center in New York, the true first floor could be underground, where more shops line the bustling arcades than are found on street level.

The Villa Stein was concrete. The roof was flat and meant for use as still another floor. Once we reached it and faced east, we were rewarded with the wonderful panorama of Paris. The Eiffel Tower, the towers of Notre Dame, and the Arc de Triomphe, where the ride started, rose up some twelve miles away. Right below us was the villa's own small garden. It combined the best of our native back yard and front yard. This valuable space was hidden from passers-by. It was beautified like our front yard, which however, we reserve for looks and regard as too public for relaxation. The utility space or dumping ground to which we often reduce our back yard was now discreetly buried under the house proper.

Floors extended outside the walls like open decks. Matisse paintings hung on partitions that veered right and left in unexpected and apparently illogical directions. No room was a box; none even was closed in. Though passage from one to another was rarely in a straight line, at least no doors impeded it.

This house could not be viewed in isolation. It possessed a matchless approach. How much more enthusiastic was the appreciation of a visitor who reached it through two of Europe's beautiful parks, a charming village square, and along the famous Seine! Its architecture in a broad and a specific sense began twelve miles away.

Though Le Corbusier could not take credit for that, he would be the first to be aware of it. Whereabouts in the real-estate business, that is at just what stage in planning, should the architect start interfering on our behalf? Maybe the local government should help with certain regulations? Does our home lie at the end of a historic route? To reach it must we drive by the stockyards, by a grimy factory, through slums, or past an auto graveyard? At once we wish we could compel the man building a mile off to conform to general standards of looks and values. There is some control over immediate neighborhoods. The developer of a fifty-acre tract, say, may sell only to people who will erect a house of a minimum dollar value, perhaps $50,000. That does not mean it has to be handsome. It merely has to be expensive. It can be ugly. But there is no check on the second developer who turns his adjacent fifty acres into a trailer camp.

This problem occurs appropriately in connection with Le Corbusier, who has been singularly sensitive to environment. Buildings have a moral aspect, we have learned. Now we realize they have a social character. Wright designed for the single family. Le Corbusier, always attentive to the needs of the masses, designed for a town or city. Consequently, city planning is involved. This deserves a chapter by itself and will have one, but we must keep it in mind as we look at other Le Corbusier creations.

Not everyone can live near rivers, parks, and palaces. A second Le Corbusier house lies in the Paris suburb of Neuilly. As Garches promised to be, this, in fact, is closely crowded by neighbors. Thus like many city homes it could have, architecturally, only a front and a back. The sides were blanks. This Villa Cook belonged to the American expatriate painter William Cook. Like the Stein house, it had no cellar and no ground floor but did have a flat roof. The ingenious Le Corbusier really left Cook with more ground or its equivalent than he owned at the start. The roof was turned into a garden. On the actual ground area the car was parked and equipment stored; a walk led to the "front" yard in the rear; there was an entrance to the circular stairs up into the dwelling proper. The plot was twenty-five feet wide. Le Corbusier hung the entire structure on a single central steel pillar and cantilevered the floors out from it. Thus no precious space was wasted in thick supporting walls. There was a two-story living room, a favorite of Le Corbusier's. He called this his cubic house, and it was almost a cube. The cube was linked significantly to the Cubism that for two decades preoccupied avant-garde artists. Le Corbusier was himself a painter.

Man is the key to the Frenchman's work. As we walk around town to look at architecture, he walks around town to create it. "You have to walk through architecture," he said. It can never be abstract like painting. Flesh-and-blood man, not abstract man, is at the core of every house, apartment, and larger building. Le Corbusier would start with this living creature, lift him from his chair, guide him out the door, downstairs to the street, and out to the country. Thus architecture is a walk. All the proportions of the visual and physical experience in which this symbolic man participated would be of the essence of architecture. Wright made somewhat the same profession, but Le Corbusier worked more consciously and consistently within the theory. Wright was more interested in fitting the building to the setting. Le Corbusier fitted it to social man, to mankind. Thus he arrived at his Modulor.

All is of course a matter of proportion, as in a painting. Some shapes do not go together; some lengths clash within the same picture frame. Le Corbusier complained of a certain building that it was perhaps made for a flea or a giraffe but never for a man. His module derived from man, cut at the waist for one dimension, arm raised overhead for another, and subdivided as need arose. There can thus be absolutely mathematical relations between all the parts. A step may be a tenth of a module, a door a module and a half; a room is three modules; one building stands ten modules from another. As Wright marked some buildings with a little red initialed square to show "I, Wright" had been there, Le Corbusier stamped into the concrete—as at his Marseille apartment—the muscular, powerful image of his Modulor with the proportions nicked off like inches on a ruler. It is like the key to a cypher. It is a trademark. It is a basis for regularity. What can go too wrong if one is always faithful to the system?

Man has often dreamed there was some dependable key to beauty. The English artist Hogarth identified the S-curve or a modification of it with inevitable pure beauty. While Phidias and his pair of architects, Ictinus and Callicrates, were consummate geniuses, theorists hunt for more to explain the Parthenon, that Doric glory and perfection on the Acropolis. So they decide the Greeks laid down arbitrarily as their module a fraction of a magnificent pillar. It or its multiple became their guiding dimension. Or the secret of the grandeur of temple and pyramid lay in the Golden Mean, or Golden Section, an abstract and rigid system of proportions. At some point, most of these theories, matched exactly against the monuments, can apparently be proved false. If Wright and Le Corbusier relied on a module, no doubt it served as a check. It guarded against dangerous extremes. Yet the beauty in their creations was more in the man and his genius than in the theory, more magical than geometrical.

Le Corbusier's studio and living quarters occupied two floors of an apartment in Boulogne, another Paris suburb.

The space was not cluttered—perhaps a low stand, a chair, and table contrasted with Wright's ponderous and nearly immovable furniture. There was an easel for his Cubist paintings. The occupant was very conscious of American mechanical superiority. He did not hesitate to admit it to us or to scoff at his countrymen. On his seventh and eighth floors, as he said, "I live at an altitude of seventy-two feet while my friend [the American architect Wallace K.] Harrison works at a height of eight hundred and twenty feet in Rockefeller Center. And when we take the elevator at the same moment we arrive at our doors at the same time, in forty-five seconds."

Le Corbusier not only traveled about his own city of Neuchâtel but also abroad. Born in 1887 in Switzerland, he was still young when he toured the chief architectural sites along the northern Mediterranean. He studied the Parthenon and its relation to the rock of the Acropolis, the sea, and the mountains.

Le Corbusier, shortened in professional circles to Corbu, was named Charles Edouard Jeanneret at birth. His father and mother engraved watch cases in Switzerland. After local study, he was awarded a commission to build a house when he was only eighteen. In his view, he was never properly educated, and he hoped other beginners would have the advantage denied him. What more he could have accomplished than he did is impossible to imagine, however, and some of his fellows with even less formal schooling preferred it that way.

Like them, he learned by doing. In Germany, he got a job with Peter Behrens, among whose employees were Walter Gropius and Mies van der Rohe of Bauhaus fame. A second influence on Le Corbusier was Joseph Hoffmann of Vienna. For a little over a year he worked—his word "slaved" was no doubt accurate—for Auguste Perret in Paris. He was formed directly and basically by the concrete techniques studied under Perret, twenty years his senior, early master of the fascinating semifluid medium. The very idea of "pouring" a building thrilled him. This was marvelous stuff. As cake batter fits the pan, as toothpaste fits the tube, concrete fitted the unprecedented ideas that thronged Le Corbusier's mind.

His idea that a house is a machine intrigued some people and irritated others—he was particularly successful at rallying friends to his cause and stirring up bands of enemies. A house should be as efficient as a bicycle or typewriter: no cornices, no cellar, no gimcracks. Everything must contribute immediately to efficient riding, typing, and living. Old values and old definitions served no purpose any more: "A wall no longer needs to carry weight; a house has every interest in being off the ground . . . no longer needs a pitched roof; it can be made in a factory."

This tended to eliminate carpenter, bricklayer, and roofer. They emphatically wanted not to be eliminated and attacked Le Corbusier. Their charges were based not on the loss of their jobs but on the false ground that his houses were no good. As representatives of powerful labor unions, they did a lot of harm. Le Corbusier was also accused of Communist sympathies. Frank Lloyd Wright, ordinarily not so gullible, lent himself to the criticism of his politics. Wright must have realized that politics, like morals, had nothing to do with architecture. A good house is a good house whether it is built by or for a Democrat, a Republican, or a robber baron, whether it stands in Moscow, Peiping, or New York. The basic obstacle to Le Corbusier was the conservative and academic mind. Perret was accepted as a member of the Beaux-Arts faculty. But to counteract his modernist influence, his students, in order to graduate, had to finish their courses under a conventional professor. The man without ideas ruled the man with. Half a century after the trade accepted concrete, the Beaux-Arts still did no original work in it. Marble alone was the historic, official medium in the official opinion of faculty members—who to be consistent should still have been writing with a quill pen by candlelight and riding horseback to class.

The Savoye House of forty years ago incorporated most of Le Corbusier's fresh ideas. It began one floor up. It rested on pillars, which, to be sure, stood free as they had throughout the past. But used thus like stilts, they are defined by the French word *pilotis*. Skeleton frame and walls were separate, each performing its own distinctive function. Rooms ran into one another freely. Le Corbusier liked walls to bend and weave. Sometimes he curved them oddly around a tub in the bathroom or gave them a capricious S-twist to accommodate a grand piano in the drawing room. The roof was flat for garden and lounge. There were ribbon windows. Now deteriorated badly, the Savoye is best studied, like Wright's Robie House, in a model in the Museum of Modern Art in New York. Threatened with destruction after the war, the original was saved by France's alert minister for Cultural Affairs, André Malraux. In the same way, Germany's Bonn government has preserved an early factory by Walter Gropius. Americans save some monuments, too, though more often by private means, like the gift of Fallingwater to the nonprofit Western Pennsylvania Conservancy. Both processes are haphazard; the wrecker's ball has knocked down many irreplaceable treasures.

If we had to lose all modern architects except one or two, which would we save? This is a silly game, but it is often played. The two would be Wright and Le Corbusier. Both true moderns and international figures, they design from the inside out, the purposeful inside out. There are differences. One is European, the other American; one Old World and the other New. Le Corbusier is a painter but not Wright. Le Corbusier is a city man, Wright a country fellow. Le Corbusier builds up high in a shape unrelated to the lay of the land. Wright builds low and snuggles his work into a background. Le Corbusier thinks; Wright feels. One relies on an arithmetical process, the other on organic growth.

They have another thing in common: personal and professional antagonists. Work on a private house is private business. Though it can start disputes, they are not usually advertised. But Le Corbusier busy on public construction was drawn into a lot of mean, nasty scraps. They were waged in the academy, in the anterooms of officialdom, and in the newspapers. He was just as ready to air his grievances as Wright.

In 1925, at the International Exposition of Decorative Arts in Paris, he built the Pavillon de L'Esprit Nouveau, or the New Spirit Pavilion. It was a cube with the middle cut out. The extension of the house walls proper shielded the adjacent garden. Exposition authorities did their best to show it in the worst light. They allotted it a bad spot and blocked access by practically surrounding it with an eighteen-foot fence. The judges would have awarded it first prize, but the one Frenchman among them vetoed this honor. Yet like Sullivan's Transportation Building in Chicago, it was the structure longest remembered, in part for the design, for the Le Corbusier furniture, and for the very attacks made on it with such prejudice. At the 1937 Paris World's Fair, Le Corbusier suffered similar ill treatment; his work was located where it was sure to be demolished the minute the show closed.

He built some fifty houses of reinforced concrete for the working class in Pessac, a Bordeaux suburb. According to his indignant account, local contractors and architects tried their hardest to obstruct the project. Unfriendly officialdom barred occupancy for three years. Despite representations to the mayor, the prefect, and the water company, Pessac was deliberately deprived of a water supply for six years. It reversed a curious situation in Berlin where workers would not move into modern homes, sentimentally preferring the old dilapidated tenements to the new, cheaper, and more efficient ones.

But more trouble was brewing in Paris—his headquarters, his home, the place where his heart was, the place that most persistently bedeviled him. The design for a studio for a fellow painter and architect, Amédée Ozenfant, was no problem at all. The Salvation Army Building, though, offered the city an excuse to interfere. It jumped at the chance and prevented numerous refinements. The Swiss Pavilion at the Cité Universitaire, or University City, embodied Le Corbusier's methods and design and many novelties. Added together, they caused him more headaches. This is an important sight in present-day Paris. One of the original vertical-slab structures, it provides a preview of the huge one for the United Nations on the East River in New York. A five-story building, like an up-ended monster shoebox or domino, it rides on handsome bunched *pilotis*. Surfaces contrast richly inside and out, on floors and in walls: rubblestone, stone veneer, glass, and concrete. This slab does not fit into its environment or merge or harmonize. The terms that describe Wright do not apply. This is one thing; the surroundings are another. Le Corbusier made exactly what he wanted first, then only second set it in its destined place. If it looked like a sore thumb sticking up out of the ground, it was a marvelous and unprecedented sore thumb. Officials disapproved of everything about it. They hoped Le Corbusier would accept the gift of seeds for vines to grow and cover the rubblestone. To hide the obnoxious surfaces even more, they planted shrubs. His theory ran absolutely counter to theirs. This was not only a confrontation of contrasting personalities; it was also a fundamental ideological difference. His wall instead of sinking into the background must stand out from it. It was man-made. He insisted that it show it.

He has been called a poor loser. He could rip into accusers with a savagery sometimes excessive and, for a reasoning man, unreasonable. But his foes had themselves to blame. They egged him on; they ganged up on him; they attacked him when he was leaving them alone. He was utterly nonconformist. He took nothing for granted. He must always be asking why and how and wherefore. The man whose buildings were a brand-new sight spoke with a brand-new voice. He put us in his debt and at the same time riled some tempers by his fresh and unspoiled look at our world. Consider, for instance, his criticism of transatlantic liners. It was sparked in particular by a ship of which the French, his adopted people, were loudly boasting in the 1930's, the French Line's flagship, the glamorous Blue-Ribbon winner, *Normandie.* Instead of taking us down to the sea, Le Corbusier charged, it separated us from it. It was designed and operated to deceive us into thinking we were still ashore:

"You have to go on deck to look for the sea. The main deck is not very helpful: it is a covered walk barricaded by thick wooden panels. . . . It should be possible to see the superb machinery by means of properly arranged mirrors. There should be available popularizing marine instruments which would allow some participation in the activities of the bridge. . . . A library which would enable you to enter into marine interests: voyages, adventures, ship building, conquests. Public rooms and cabins done in nautical architecture and not by 'interior decorators.' Why this dissimulation, this equivocation, this hypocrisy through which the passenger is made to feel that he is still in the Place de l'Opéra [a fashionable square in Paris] or at Vichy [a watering place]?"

Business might consider it sound advertising to hire an architect who had figured on front pages as the target for attack. In some fields, any reputation good or bad is good. Le Corbusier often rated headline space both in praise and in condemnation. He began to get in the news here and abroad some forty years ago with plans for the League of Nations in Geneva. The buildings still stand there imposingly by the side of the lake. The Le Corbusier touch is missing. They are about as modern as our National Gallery in Washington or the Metropolitan Museum in New York with its magnificent and exhausting flights of stairs.

Designs for this center of world government in Geneva and the once shining hope for world peace were submitted by three hundred and seventy-seven contestants. Among them were Le Corbusier and his cousin Pierre Jeanneret. A six-man international jury appeared to favor this pair and their revolutionary four-part plan. It proposed an office building, library, meeting rooms, and a wedge-shaped assembly somewhat like the one for the later United Nations in New York. Three modernists among the judges voted for Le Corbusier and Jeanneret. One modernist and two others voted against; the opposing modernist was Baron Victor Horta, *Art Nouveau* practitioner. This disheartening tie followed sixty-five sessions of the jury. In despair, it turned the knotty matter back to the League of Nations, that is, back to the politicians. The decision embittered Le Corbusier. The

League did not behave badly. It modified the ground rules to help resolve the tie. Not politicians but architectural professionals messed it up. They rejected the second design submitted by Le Corbusier and Jeanneret in favor of a conventional and "safe" solution.

Le Corbusier again was slighted in the construction of the United Nations. The assembled governments, aware of the well-advertised rivalries, autocratically passed over the chief controversial figures, Wright and Le Corbusier. Since Wright did not function at his best in the city, his rejection could perhaps be justified. There might also be some point in not assigning this exacting task to Le Corbusier. Despite his unarguable genius, he was not familiar with processes and routines in the country where the work must be done. He himself, appreciating this handicap, praised the selection of Wallace K. Harrison, who had had the invaluable experience of designing the even larger Rockefeller Center. Traces of Le Corbusier can be spotted in the background—even the foreground—of that dramatic group rising between First Avenue and the East River. Details of the assembly hall are reminders of the Frenchman. The tall slab of the Secretariat was his stepchild. He would, in fact, charge the theft of specific ideas from his sketchbook.

Perhaps he would have done a sounder job. An entrance is too elaborate. He would have simplified. He might have figured out a wiser orientation. If the slab's long all-glass sides had faced north and south, they would have sacrificed views of the East River and the skyline. But facing east and west, though they enjoy the views, they take a beating from the direct rays of the sun morning and afternoon. This city has stifling high temperatures three months every year. Le Corbusier might have known better how to keep down the cost of air conditioning and fuel.

When the United Nations Educational, Scientific, and Cultural Organization, or UNESCO, wanted designs for its Paris headquarters, it outfoxed the Frenchman. He was appointed to the board, which, in turn, was to appoint the architects. Their good choices were Marcel Breuer, Pier Luigi Nervi, and Bernard Zehrfuss.

This reads like a record of disappointments and failures. But Le Corbusier had his triumphs. One was the chapel of Notre Dame du Haut in Ronchamp. Dating in the 1950's, it is as expressionist as the trolley and plow and tank shapes metamorphosed a few decades earlier into offices and factories. The windows are spotted about apparently at random. The huge curly-edge roof resembles a boy's high-riding cap. The stone towers have concrete tops. Le Corbusier's colors are deep red and purple. The body of the church is quiet and subdued, and the mood is domestic, rustic, or pastoral, if not always clearly religious.

According to Le Corbusier, no building in France except the châteaux along the Loire River attracted more visitors than his Unité d'Habitation, his tenement complex, in Marseille. It was finished in 1952. It consists of a huge ferroconcrete box four hundred and fifty feet long and sixty-five feet through, mounted on wedgelike *pilotis*. Into it, as if it were a bureau, were slid, somewhat like drawers, scores of apartments to accommodate more than a thousand people. They are two-story units, Le Corbusier's favorite form. His deep sun breakers temper the Mediterranean heat. Light and shadow vary interestingly across the inset balconies and concrete honeycomb on the front facing the sea. The concrete is left rough.

This is a separate, distinct village. Instead of sprawling greedily over a lot of land, it is lifted into the air. The main shopping street is in the center of town as we would expect;

that means halfway up. Here the residents buy groceries, have their laundry done, or relax with a glass of wine in a café. In a similar later apartment in Nantes, Le Corbusier located the market at ground level in the hope of more needed business from outside. Marseille people who do their own washing hang it on the front balconies to dry. It has been complained that some bedrooms are narrow and apartments do not get enough light. Almost two hundred feet up, the roof, utilized like so much more ground, offers a splendid view of mountains and sea. A wide lawn separates the rear from street noises and smells. This Unité d'Habitation may have no mayor, no police chief, no school superintendent—though it has a nursery. There are no extra roads to build, clean, or clear of snow, no parking problem, no traffic cops, and comparatively only a few yards, not miles, of water mains and power and phone lines.

The place stands on the edge of Marseille. It is not far from the picturesque Old Port, a tourist mecca and birthplace of the great caricaturist and painter Honoré Daumier. Road builders as grasping in France as they are here schemed to carve a wide highway through this historic area. It was spared in part by the efforts of Le Corbusier, too often unjustly accused of scrapping the old for the sake of the new. Pink stone brightens the ancient waterfront fortifications. There are dozens of quaint fishing boats. Notre Dame de la Garde towers above the scene. We circle it on the cliff-edge road high above the water to reach Le Corbusier's prize apartment. The colorful approach can be compared with that to the Villa Stein in Garches.

There is also Le Corbusier's great construction in India at Chandigarh—too far away for most of us to visit. Here was a rare challenge: an entire community of houses and government buildings. Two English architects, Maxwell Fry and

Jane Drew, both members of the International Congress of Modern Architecture of which Le Corbusier had been a founder, were associated with him. The city, on the plain below the Himalayas, has two rainy months and ten hot ones. The general layout provided roads and walks for different purposes: pedestrians, cyclists, shoppers afoot and in cars, and speeding traffic. Some individual homes were erected at a cost under $700. The four-story court, rather like a cave, has an open entrance, ramps, and sun breakers all intended to permit freer circulation of air and lower the temperatures. Court-room sounds that might echo from concrete walls are absorbed by tapestries by Le Corbusier. Besides problems due to climate and the need to economize, there was the task of putting up a modern building with untrained labor—Wright had the same handicap in Japan. Steel and concrete cost money in India; only brick was cheap and handmade. But on what concrete he did use the marks of the boards remained as they had at Marseille. This is a characteristic of the New Brutalism, as it is called. Concrete no longer even suggests marble. It is pure concrete to sight and touch.

What we now detect signs of in Marseille, in the Swiss Pavilion, in Chandigarh, is the International Style. Its chief exponent is Mies van der Rohe. He is a formidable rival of both Le Corbusier and Wright for a place in the forefront. All three are equally committed to modern materials. But Mies is the simplest, most direct, the purest geometer of them all. Le Corbusier has been the midway figure.

12 | Ludwig Mies van der Rohe

The give and take in the cultural fields in Europe brought the artist and the architect together. Frank Lloyd Wright might deny this association—and he erected a museum for paintings that, as critics charged, had little to do with painting. But abroad, abstract ideas recorded on canvas had a look astonishingly like some new homes or offices. Painters did not paint buildings; architects did not build paintings. Nevertheless, two-dimensional assemblages of lines and masses often suggested three-dimensional assemblages of walls, planes, and beams. Which came first is not so important as the fact they are blood relations.

A sketch of the planes of a Prairie House would have

seemed like a very salable piece of art indeed to a Paris gallery dealing, say, in Mondrian abstractions. Piet Mondrian created paintings out of a few lines sparsely arranged across a canvas. An architectural design is a few lines sparsely arranged across heavy-duty paper. Mondrian's art, in association with that of another theorist and painter, Théo van Doesburg, is classified under the name *de Stijl. De Stijl* was "style," and it was also a magazine. The young Dutchman J. J. P. Oud, later the architect for the city of Rotterdam, is remembered in particular for one building, the Café de Unie. For its façade, he adapted the cover design of the magazine *De Stijl,* in effect upending it. The words are different, it is a good deal bigger, but he employed the same or similar colors and spacing. In a like manner, advertising artists frequently adapt the style of a museum artist for their layouts. *De Stijl* printed an ingenious diagram showing how slight were the touches needed in lines and spaces to pass from one art form to another. The sequence illustrated was from sculpture to chair to magazine cover to a house design.

Ludwig Mies van der Rohe sponsored a similar avant-garde magazine in Germany: *G* from the word *Gestaltung,* meaning the creative force. The interchange among painting, sculpture, and architecture was cleverly summarized in one issue by Van Doesburg. He disposed four black squares in an asymmetrical pattern to represent the painting. Turned into cubes, they became sculpture. With further modifications of their surfaces, they grew into buildings. The arts are cousins. This cousinship is reassuring. We might suspect the painter, if we saw him alone, or the architect or the sculptor of just trying to be smart or different, of giving us not art but a sales pitch. But this is not chance, not publicity seeking, not anything but sincere creation. Squares into houses or houses into squares—one is as likely to be true as the other.

The direct transition from Wright's rectangular design to the geometrical style abroad that parallelled it, or coincided with it, might have been possible. But Europeans did not have to hunt so far for influences. The experimental and exploratory spirit, spread out wide among them, embraced the entire field of the arts. Walter Gropius' Bauhaus—the famous school that combined instruction in architecture, engineering, painting, and the crafts—was a part of it and a consequence of it. At the end of the path followed by Mies van der Rohe, there developed ultimately the International Style.

Germany bubbled over with fresh ideas when Mies was young and susceptible. In Holland on an architectural assignment, he encountered still more. In his own country, he had worked with Peter Behrens, who occupied a position analagous to Louis Sullivan's among us. Starting in 1906, Behrens stirred the admiration of the profession with buildings erected out of two overlapping disciplines: architecture and engineering. His best known structure was the Berlin turbine factory for the electrical industry known as AEG. That monumental work had plain walls, plain windows, and nice proportions. The breadth of Behrens' functions is as significant and modern as his style. In addition to the architecture and engineering, he controlled all design work including advertising layouts and packaging.

Mies was born in Aachen in 1886. His family was poor. His father, a mason, cut stone for a living. The son added his mother's name, van der Rohe, to the father's, Mies. Like Wright, he received no formal training. The best he could manage was a couple of years in a trade school. At fifteen, he was a draftsman for small-time architects. He did menial work at construction sites. As he recalled, "We had to go out and get boiling water for the carpenters framing in the roof. . . . They used water to make coffee, and if we didn't get the water fast enough, they would throw one of their sharp axes after us to make us hurry up." Even if they had not hounded this youngster, carpenters would be a vanishing tribe. But presumably he never went out of his way to create work for them.

Besides apprenticeship to several architects around Aachen, he spent some time with Bruno Paul, the furniture designer. At twenty-one, only three years later than Le Corbusier, Mies turned out a house all on his own, basically traditional and surprisingly competent. During World War I, he wore the uniform of an engineer. Lacking a college degree in a period when caste ruled, he was never promoted to officer.

Madame H. E. L. J. Kröller, of the famous Kröller art collection, told him she wanted a large house in The Hague. It never went beyond the design stage. In developing it, however, he initiated a practice he continued in this country. The house was erected full-scale in a wood-and-canvas model. That alone would show how it would look in its final form on its actual site; but it was less for Madame Kröller's benefit than for his. In the United States, he moved into a barn or something bigger for similar mock-ups of parts or wholes.

The trip to Holland also introduced him to Hendrik Petrus Berlage. This Ruskin follower, like Sullivan, allowed no element of a building to play a false role. If a wall was a supporting wall, it must look it. An honest, frank support was worthy of itself and should not be hidden.

In the early 1920's, influenced profoundly by *De Stijl, Art Nouveau,* and Russian Constructivism and Suprematism, Mies produced five buildings. Though they were only on paper, they placed him in the vanguard. They keep him there today forty years later. In the 1890's, Wright had designed, again only on paper, a ten-story slab building with the façade solid glass and metal. It was one of the first such curtain walls to be proposed. Since Mies probably never saw the Wright design, he, too, deserves credit for helping to stamp on modern architecture a form and style still predominant. His project consisted of a trio of twenty-story towers centered around a utility area for elevators, heating, and the usual services. The street surfaces from the ground clear to the top were nothing but glass.

Another two of Mies's proposals were glass, and as has been remarked, nothing "could be more 'glass'." There were no cornices, and the top was cut off flat. This was fishbowl architecture. Mies's biographer and later partner, Philip C. Johnson, would build himself a famous all-glass home in Connecticut.

The next project, an office building, was rather engineering than architecture. The floors were cantilevered from heavy columns. As at Fallingwater and the Guggenheim Museum, the outer edges were folded up as part of the outer wall. The rest was miles of ribbon windows. Mies called this "skin and bone architecture." This led Théo van Doesburg to dub him an "anatomical architect." This is basically the International Style. It is doing the mostest with the leastest. The building ends at the top in a thin projecting slab. The entrance, instead of being a separate feature, was merely an interruption of the window and turned-up wall. A broad flight of steps cuts into the interior, revealing the rows of massive columns. Office buildings today look more like this than like any other pioneering design. If an architect cannot pull something brand-new out of his sleeve, he almost certainly resorts to Mies's strong, plain, unadorned parallels of ribbon glass and tucked-up floor edges.

His fifth project was a country house of reinforced concrete. The purpose was the separation of the various functions—as Olmsted kept one kind of traffic off the heels of another in the park. Mies wanted them pigeonholed so that the work of the kitchen, living room, dining room, and so on could continue without hindering what took place in the others. The result is the "zoned house."

As early as 1925, he showed a liking for brick. He chose it for his monument to Karl Liebknecht and Rosa Luxemburg, the proletarian leaders. Its virtues were the standard size and the interesting patterns it lent itself to. It was an honest medium, all that it seemed to the glance to be. The Berlage disciple welcomed this four-square quality. The roughness, even crudity of the surface that offended some other modernists was a big part of its appeal.

In 1927, the association of German architects under his direction contributed to the city of Stuttgart exhibition. He planned a community all of one piece spread along a sloping site. Instead of streets, there were to be squares entered by walks rather than roadways. But the city had hoped to sell individual units and doubted it could find buyers for an entire street or town. So Mies acquiesced and provided the handy salable article. To secure a representative cross section of contemporary work, he invited his most celebrated colleagues to supply designs. Among them were Le Corbusier, as we have noted, and Gropius, Oud, and Behrens. If either Wright or Le Corbusier had bossed the show, it has been suggested wryly but with justice, each would have hogged the entire job himself. Such virtuosos would refuse to share the spotlight.

Even world's fairs, despite the diversified talent they draw on, rarely display work so modern or advance its cause so successfully as did these men at the Stuttgart exhibition.

Philip C. Johnson: The remodeled and enlarged *Museum of Modern Art,*
New York City, the façade facing the sculpture garden.
  [Photo by Alexandre Georges, courtesy, The Museum of Modern Art, New York]

ABOVE   Eero Saarinen: *Dulles International Airport,* Washington, D. C., showing the terminal and flight tower.

    [*Courtesy, Federal Aviation Agency*]

RIGHT   R. Buckminster Fuller and Frits W. Went: *The Climatron,* St. Louis, Missouri.

    [*Courtesy, Hedrich-Blessing and Downtown in St. Louis, Inc.*]

LEFT   Othmar H. Ammann: *Verrazano-Narrows Bridge,* from Staten Island looking toward Brooklyn, N. Y.

[*Courtesy, Triborough Bridge and Tunnel Authority*]

ABOVE   Skidmore, Owings & Merrill—Gordon Bunshaft: *Beinecke Rare Book and Manuscript Library,* Yale University, New Haven, Connecticut, with the rim of the Isamu Noguchi sunken sculpture garden directly before it.

[*Courtesy, Yale University News Bureau*]

LEFT   Wallace K. Harrison: *First Presbyterian Church,* Stamford, Connecticut.

  [*Courtesy, Fennar Studio, Stamford*]

ABOVE   Sir Basil Spence: *Cathedral Church of St. Michael,* Coventry, England, southeast wall, with Sir Jacob Epstein's bronze of *St. Michael and the Dragon* beside the porch, to the left, and the Baptistery window immediately to the right.

  [*Courtesy, British Travel Association*] ___

Clover-leaf intersection of New Jersey Highways 4 and 17, west of the George Washington Bridge.

[*Courtesy, Standard Oil Company (New Jersey)*]

Though the men differed, the similarities were more important than the differences. They were working in the same decade with the same materials under the same general guiding principles. Thus, as in exhibits of painting and performances of music, an inevitable sameness resulted. These new practitioners raised the wall that was no more than a curtain. They were chary of ornament, relying mainly on the color and texture of materials to vary the surfaces. Unlike Gaudi and Richardson, they felt no deep concern for sculptural quality. The inside dictated to the outside. Instead of balancing the elements of a building, they were more apt to contrast them—like the modernist at his easel preoccupied not with balance but with dynamic asymmetry, with the thrust of diagonals. The new painting was a sort of cantilever in oil on canvas.

Mies's motto is, "Less is more." It accurately describes his work, plain, unadorned, starkly reduced to posts, roof, and a base to stand on. "Less is more" fits the International Style equally well.

Two years after Stuttgart, Mies constructed what has be called the most beautiful building anywhere. He got commission for the German Pavilion at the Internationa position in Barcelona. It was purely for display, not t some exhibits but to show off. It did not include e ubiquitous essential, the utility core. It was a cou decorative shell-like shelters in public parks. Ano tage Mies enjoyed was plenty of money. Thoug deck it with jewels, he chose some luxurious materials: marble, chromium plate, glass, o manship was faultless, too, a Mies charac an ideal assemblage of flat planes, horizo overhead and vertical in between. Oc were extended, idly as it seemed. The

pair of reflecting pools and a statue by the German Georg Kolbe. This is plain and simple; this is for no purpose at all and yet for every purpose, a universal building. It could not be closer to abstract. Mies is the impersonal builder. There is Wright in a Prairie House, and Le Corbusier in a Swiss Pavilion or a Unité d'Habitation. But Mies eliminates Mies almost completely. In the barest planes and the cleanest spaces, it is easy to read International Stylist but hard to read specifically Mies.

The Tugendhat House in Brno, Czechoslovakia, was so generalized and universalized that it amounted principally to one room. But the room had the dimensions of a hall: fifty by eighty feet. Walls of onyx and ebony marked off but did not separate the dining room, living room, library, and entryway. It suggested a revolving stage with all the scenes mounted in advance, except that we moved from one to another in the house while they spin around to confront us in the theater. Outside walls were glass. In case even glass seemed to interfere with the view, the push of a button sent the panels sliding into the floor. The inside swept out; the outside swept in, with nothing to hinder. (In an apartment on a Champs-Elysées rooftop, Le Corbusier mounted shrubs on an elevator; a push button dropped them out of sight and opened up a Paris vista.)

In general, Mies's building, which employs panels and posts most sparingly, resembles a child's play with plywood sections and dowels, or plywood alone. Or it is like a house of cards, though it is intended to endure. Lay one flat; balance two or three at amusing or intriguing angles atop it edgewise; cover with another one or two. There, you are an architect! What's more, you are an architect in the International Style. Until the last few years, this style has predominated in this country.

Some architects build your house and let you carry on. Some build your house and design your furniture. Mies went a step farther: built the house, designed the furniture, and told you to the inch where it had to be put and where it had to stay. Does this detract from homeyness? People who have lived in a Mies house like it his way. Some of us might object to this rigidity. We might prefer the informality of a Le Corbusier interior with furniture that can be shoved around at our caprice rather than at our builder's orders. Mies, to be sure, if he must be unyielding, had a remarkable chair to be unyielding about. The Barcelona chair, so-called, was of bent tubular steel with cantilevered seat and floor rest. The Museum of Modern Art in New York exhibits one.

In 1930, Mies was appointed director of the Bauhaus. The Nazis were coming into power in Germany. As they hated modern art, they hated modern architecture, the Bauhaus itself, and, in particular, its new head. They had scorned and ridiculed the epochal community at Stuttgart. They attacked the Bauhaus as Bolshevistic and degenerate. Communists controlled it briefly, it is true. But its faculty included Paul Klee, Herbert Bayer, Josef Albers, Lyonel Feininger, and Vassily Kandinsky. No institution in the world came near matching that galaxy of teachers. The operation was transferred to Berlin, where in 1933 Mies talked with Alfred Rosenberg. The Nazi chief granted him permission to carry on. Mies realized this meant only a temporary respite from persecution. He reported to his colleagues that he was closing the historic school.

Like Gropius, he went to England for only a short time. Then in 1938, he came to the United States, where he has lived and practiced since. Official circles here were cool. They remembered the Communist associations at the Bauhaus and the monument reverently erected to the memory of the leftist Liebknecht and Luxemburg. Opposition ended when designs started pouring from his studio. Philip C. Johnson had suggested a project in Wyoming. Though that fell through, it led to his introduction to an official of Armour Institute, later the Illinois Institute of Technology. Mies was asked to head the architectural department. Soon afterward the commission for the new campus was awarded to him.

An assignment of this magnitude constitutes a tremendous challenge and a nearly unique opportunity. Few men have the luck to leave their mark on such a sizable project. The assigned area was cut by a central street. Mies wanted to eliminate it and plan more freely within the single larger space. The street had to stay. With two halves to deal with when he preferred a whole, with an unwanted symmetry forced on him, he grouped his buildings around squares, much as at Stuttgart. He treated the big over-all lot like a small interior, nicely varying the closed and open spaces. Proportion was all. The secret of the resulting orderliness lies, in part, in his twenty-four-foot module. It could be increased to a twenty-four by twenty-four-foot square and a twenty-four by twenty-four by twelve-foot solid. This governs interior dimensions and the distances between buildings.

The design for the library and administration building has been praised as possibly his greatest. The plan is a rectangle, undecorated. He did not want the building to look architectural. The effect he aimed at has been described as "the absence of architecture." It might be a reversion to Wright's organic growth. There were to be huge glass panels at the entrance. Offices in administration quarters were separated only by eight-foot-high partitions, without ceilings—this works only with expert soundproofing, as lesser architects have inadvertently demonstrated. Above them and between them and the roof three stories up, a mezzanine grandly branched out from a central pier.

Steel beams outside, not inside, hold the building up, somewhat as a roadway hangs from the cables of a bridge— Mies managed this more obviously and dramatically in a restaurant much more like a bridge. Four corner columns support steel trusses from which the roof is suspended. This reminds us of Le Corbusier's daring sketch for a façade swung from a soaring arch on a Moscow project. It reminds us, too, of the arch pure and simple, symbolical instead of practical, designed by Eero Saarinen to symbolize the Gateway to the West in St. Louis. The roof support may be inside or out. Mies dramatized its function and pointed out exactly how he used it—no trick, no magic—by putting it where it could be seen. He tagged it: this is frame, this is bone, all else is skin.

His famous apartments known as "860" on the Lakeshore Drive in Chicago were planned as steel-frame jobs. The local building code required a two-inch concrete covering. This would have created rows of rectangles and a squat and dumpy look instead of a soaring, flying one. Mies applied black steel plates, treated them as his concrete mold, left them on, and stiffened them by welding to them vertical I-beam rails eight inches thick. They climb handsomely two hundred and fifty feet to the roof. They are wonderfully decorative, but decoration is subordinate.

These plates and I-beam mullions appear on perhaps his finest work and one of his latest, the Seagram Building on Park Avenue in New York. The daughter of Seagram's president was in Paris when she saw some proposed designs for a new center. Since she did not approve of them, she hurried home to say so. Converting her father to her point of view, she set out on a hunt for the firm capable of the distinguished work they both envisaged. She considered Wright and Le Corbusier, among others. Introduced by Philip C. Johnson to Mies, she decided he was the man. Johnson was associated with him on the project.

The building covering an entire block front reaches far back toward Lexington Avenue. A thirty-eight-story tower, handsome and dignified, rises from a wide, deep granite plaza. The approach is flanked by two shallow rectangular pools. The original slender perpendicular streams of water that shoot up from them harmonized with the height behind them, but because of the gusty wind they may have splattered some passers-by; now the fountains are much lower and less effective, too, unhappily. The entrance leads into arcades almost thirty feet high. One prime virtue is color. The glass is reflecting, and the steel is bronzed. It is a most pleasant relief after all the gray of Rockefeller Center and up and down Park Avenue and the off-white of Lincoln Center.

When the project was broached, New York authorities discovered that Mies lacked a state license. When he applied, he informed them incidentally that he had not finished high school. This seemed to the official mind to weigh more against him than the Illinois Institute campus and other outstanding, world-renowned achievements counted for him. Incensed at this bigotry, Mies was ready to quit when Johnson intervened successfully.

Preliminary troubles were more than matched by those after the event. If the Seagram had been another ordinary utility-type skyscraper, hogging overhead light and every inch of ground legally allowable, the tax assessor would have treated it routinely. But a supertax was slapped on the supervalues of spacing, finishing, taste, workmanship, and beauty. Assessors set a higher tax rate, on the grounds that good looks are a tangible value. Of course they never set a lower rate on an ugly building. The owners' suit to overturn the decision has encountered some judicial hostility. The court charged Seagram with wastefulness in not using all the space available. The attractive Pepsi-Cola building ten blocks farther north has been subjected to the same harrying tactic. New York City is saying: We welcome run-of-the-mill architects and penalize good ones. You may favor the embellishment of your streets and avenues, but we shall prevent it if we can.

The Seagram is, in fact, worth all the more because Park Avenue cries out for sound, modern, handsome architectural features. It has been dammed up just above Forty-second Street by the gigantism of the Pan Am Building set astride Grand Central Terminal. The once sedate and spacious avenue now deteriorates into a great boxed canyon. It is lined monotonously by double rows of gray hives with little color and little variation in texture and pattern. They are all stolidly geometric and practical and a tremendous bore to the eye. One other earlier building helps importantly to redeem this blight: Lever House not far above Seagram on the opposite side. The work of Skidmore, Owings & Merrill, it, in effect, starts at the second floor. The ground area is left open mostly for tasteful planting and as a promenade. Tall and svelte, Lever House turns glass façades south, east, and north and considerately leaves some light and air for the neighbors.

Mies is almost as indifferent as Le Corbusier to site. We might wish he paid as much attention to why he builds as to how. Instead, he prefers all-purpose containers, interchangeable like the Barcelona pavilion. His principal though not his sole concern is structure. He gets closer and closer to putting up a building with less and less. As Le Corbusier works mainly with concrete, he works mainly with steel. Thus he can cut his frame or skeleton down to next to nothing: bottom, top, and the least amount possible in between. This is not skin and bone; it is bare bone alone.

The International Style has been blamed for some barren, homely stretches along our streets and avenues. We do not want to revert to Gaudi and his excesses, to Victor Horta and *Art Nouveau,* or to Expressionism. But it ought to be possible to relieve somewhat the common flat, dull appearance. We are getting perhaps more engineering than architecture. Buildings' faces need attention.

13 | New Directions

The International Style is influential, in part, because it is open and aboveboard and easy to imitate. The designer's fingerprints are not to be found. He resembles the artist whose impersonal, abstract paintings reveal the least possible amount of himself. Here is a picture, here the brush, here the painter. It is not an arm and a man moving but a belt and wheel, a drive shaft.

Should architecture become a little more personal? The house fits the hillside, fine, but how do we fit the house? Concrete was never employed more expertly, steel more frankly, but how comfortable is the place to eat and sleep and live in? Have modern methods turned the house into a home? The Statue of Liberty stands for something. Is there a symbolic value to the slab of a Secretariat at the United Nations?

Critics and architects have asked these questions. Hints of a changed direction appear here and there—in Mexico, California, St. Louis, New York, England. The architect wonders why, after all, he should not let his fingerprints show. He is not a machine that he should create machines. On the contrary, he is different as all men are. This difference is stamped on everything from his drawing board. At once other questions occur to him. In the phrase of Louis I. Kahn, "What does the building want to be?" Kahn is one of the different men. Another we shall visit is R. Buckminster Fuller, a unique blend of architect, engineer, scientist, and dreamer. Perhaps the word magician fits best. Some people salute him as the true architect of the space age.

It is not enough to let materials and methods speak. Let the man speak, too. If ever a house of ours is to say noble things, the voice of the architect himself must surely be heard. Younger practitioners wonder what is wrong with a little decoration or comfort or homeyness. Part of the stirring in the field is inevitable. Styles never last whether in construction, hats, or autos. But this is more than whim. All of a sudden architecture has been seized with a vision of potentialities not imagined before. It studies desperately how to make the most of them.

Richard Neutra in California and occasionally in Latin America usually works into his houses more comfort and ease than his fellows with their geometric rigidity. To be sure, he inhabits a beneficent and mellow climate. He does not have to guard against both five feet of snow and a hundred degrees of temperature. His well-known Lovell House in Los Angeles is dated as long ago as 1929. The reinforced concrete of the walls was sprayed from a gun. Air and light fill the place. Windows and passageways are generously large, for he wants the outside to come in.

As we might guess, he passed a season or two with Frank Lloyd Wright at Taliesin. Before settling here, he studied in his birthplace, Vienna, and in Switzerland. He shows more diversity than some other masters and welcomes a variety of problems. For many years, his own home has stood in the midst of other houses on a plot sixty by seventy feet. It has lots of windows. But thanks to their careful arrangement and to judicious planting, every one provides a view with which no nearby house interferes. He loves a view, which he believes is as healthy for a well man as for the hospital patient. On a hillside house, the balcony faces the sea. The glass wall drops down to the floor in the bedroom so anyone lying there can enjoy the seascape without stirring. Are there boulders on a proposed site? He spares them as other men spare the trees. Does he plan a pool? His glass wall lowered right down to its surface divides it in two, one half inside and one half out. A prime handicap in this country, he complains, is the lack of a native architectural tradition. He points to the fine, nice sense of the Japanese, Spanish, English, and other peoples who with no training enhance even their unimportant streets with visual satisfactions.

Alvar Aalto is another personal architect. Though he has taught as well as worked here—the Massachusetts Institute of Technology has a dormitory by him—he is seen best in his native Finland. The modules essential to some of his fellows do not figure in his designs. Born in 1898, he subscribed early to the principles embodied in the International Congress of which Le Corbusier was a founder. By 1930, without leaving home, he had been influenced by Le Corbusier and Mies. Living in a land possessing more wood than any other natural resource, he has made the most affecting and inventive use of it. He may be as long remembered for some comfortable, simply constructed chairs as for the buildings.

Steel, despite its unequaled strength, still resembles wood functionally and is employed like wood as an upright or a span. It is the stuff of post-and-lintel construction all over again. But concrete reinforced with a mesh of rods seems to perform miracles. Bridges cannot cross such chasms, roofs cannot soar so high—but they do. Out of one mold come a thousand trusses that, assembled with only semiskilled labor, raise up an enormous edifice. They can be used where they are manufactured or five thousand miles away. Concrete forms the massive *pilotis* on which Le Corbusier apartments and dormitories stand immovably. It also forms the thin skins flung high as a roof by the Mexican Felix Candela, the Spaniard Edoardo Torroja, the Italian Pier Luigi Nervi. Their buildings have to be seen to be believed—so do R. Buckminster Fuller's, the American, though fewer shapes are available by his process. We would be confident a solid mass of concrete could not be crushed by any weight. We would be just as confident a roof would collapse when spun out to less than a couple of inches thick and thrown a couple of hundred feet into the air with no external support. Yet the roof stands. That is what concrete can do. By such magic Nervi covers exhibition halls, Torroja runs cantilevers over many rows of race-track spectators. Contemporary man has created few sights so astounding and so beautiful.

An example of the principle embodied here was the canopy over the curving walk at Fallingwater. Instead of being wedged in place, it is itself a wedge. Nervi's Olympic Sports Palace in Rome, seating sixteen thousand people, is composed of sixteen hundred and twenty precast concrete sections—as a house may consist of so many thousand bricks. Its concrete dome with a span of a hundred and ninety-two feet and a three-hundred-and-fifteen-foot diameter was the largest ever when it was constructed in 1960. The two-hundred-and-ten-foot span of his earlier exhibition hall in Turin, topped with a special ferrocement of his invention— cement sprayed on a steel mesh—consisted of prefabricated vaulting sections only one and a half inches thick. Torroja has specialized in prefabricated concrete. Barrel shapes form cantilevers almost fifty feet long. They flare out over tiers of benches as jauntily as the creased cowl of a nun.

Nervi, fortunately, can be seen in New York at the city end of the George Washington Bridge. His bus terminal stretching two blocks from Fort Washington Avenue across Broadway to the bridge runway presented special problems. One street must be spanned. The ground slopes. The structure bends in the middle, since the bridge and streets are not at a right angle. Above Broadway traffic is routed around either side of a circular opening. Bus tracks trace intriguing curves, and the landing platforms are situated gracefully among them. The roof is blue concrete ramplike sections. Similar truss shapes support the outside retaining walls. Private cars speed beneath both the terminal and a row of tall skyscraper apartments.

Philip C. Johnson's pavilion for the State of New York at the World's Fair of 1964-65 illustrates the more relaxed work of the younger men—Frank Lloyd Wright designed for an amusement park, and other architects had their gayer flings. The New York Fair has added little to cultural history. The buildings serve as advertising signs rather than as architecture. Two exceptions are a fine Spanish pavilion and Johnson's—though he is better represented at the Museum of Modern Art and in the Seagram. At the Fair, he groups towers for observation and dining along with a giant pagoda as centerpiece. A roof is balanced on sixteen piers with a pair of flagpoles atop each. Low walls surround a circular floor or pit strikingly ornamented with an inset map of the state. There is a gallery—Johnson cannot be blamed for the fifth-rate entertainment that must have annoyed lots of visitors. The ceiling is red, blue, and purple.

He decorated the ceiling no less colorfully for the New York State Theater, his contribution to the Lincoln Center for the Performing Arts. Parterre and five rings of seats accommodate two thousand seven hundred people. The stage at the sides has plenty of room, as it rarely does around Times Square, where land is costly. There is no center aisle —theaters abroad often have none—but the rows are spaced comfortably apart.

Johnson, born in Cleveland in 1906, is a Harvard graduate. For years he has been director of the Department of Architecture at the Museum of Modern Art in New York. The original museum, a short way in from Fifth Avenue on a plot that extends from Fifty-third Street to Fifty-fourth, was built in 1939 by Philip L. Goodwin and Edward Durrell Stone. It gave the city its first clear idea of International Style. The interior is all wide open spaces. Partitions adjust readily to various exhibitions. This being not merely a painting gallery but a center for other cultural activities like photography, films, and architecture, it includes a small theater, a restaurant, and a beautiful garden for planting and sculpture.

With Johnson in charge, the place has been enlarged recently. The building was his toughest problem. On the rear, he was confronted by three contrasting surfaces to which he must add a not too inharmonious fourth. There were the bare style of the original; the back of Canada House, a mere service wall; and the flattened buttresses, architectural relics half a millennium out of date, on St. Thomas Church. Johnson cleverly eliminated part of these areas with trees and vines. He worked more variety into his own wall. It consists of glass, buff and white brick, and, borrowed from the Seagram, I-beam risers painted black for sharp visual accents.

The garden now lies on two levels amounting to thirty-five thousand square feet. Two large pools are lighted under water, and the whole area can be well illuminated. Sculpture is placed about. A broad flight of marble stairs provides an easy climb, aided by a smart railing with marble panels. The descent could be risky. As is too often the case, nothing distinguishes the edges of the separate steps for the visitor with faulty eyesight.

The landscape artists, Zion and Breen, no doubt with Johnson's advice, have done a model job. There are weeping birches and beeches, Lombardy poplars, and the hornbeam. Its tortured branches offer an excellent foil for the unrelieved surfaces beloved by modernists. Trees with their tops leveled off outside the restaurant suggest the lily-pad columns of Frank Lloyd Wright. Sparrows flit about in the branches.

Mexico, D.F., is fortunate in an excellent Museum of Modern Art in Chapultepec Park. It consists of a pair of buildings: an entrance or propylaea built round and a larger place to the rear along a garden path where sculpture is mounted. It is not a formal garden but a greensward or field with sparse planting of trees. A plastic dome filters light into each building. Walls of various stone textures, beautiful parquet floors of natural woods in several patterns, and an ingenious arrangement of entryway and stairs linking three levels contribute to an art center of uncommon novelty. The structures never strain for effect. Architect Pedro Ramirez Vasquez planned them admirably for exhibition purposes.

Mexican architects team up with sculptors and painters to produce more elaborate and decorative works than we in the north are accustomed to. They have a bolder sense of color —part of their Mediterranean heritage, the near-tropical setting, and the native Indian background. The famous Juan O'-Gorman library is at University City ten miles from downtown. A huge box is hoisted high in the air. Brilliant variegated mosaic covers every inch of all four sides. Here were architect and painter cooperating. They were the same person, O'Gorman cooperating with O'Gorman. Sculptors working in the gray of stone or metal turn out some eye-catching effects. One of the most productive partnerships is Herbert Hofmann-Ysenbourg, the sculptor, and Augustin Rivera Torres, the architect. Iron trellises, openwork concrete panels, statues for swimming pools and patios are common embellishments. The enormous court of the superb Museum of Anthropology is decorated not by a fountain but by a curtain of water falling from the high circular rim of the top of a giant column.

Fast-growing countries produce the most modern, as well as most of the modern, architecture. They are expanding; they need more roofs. Furthermore, they are not hampered by entrenched tradition. Or what tradition they have is so irrelevant to contemporary demands that it is ignored with impunity. Europe also has required countless more buildings than the United States. Wartime destruction forced the entire continent into a vast program of reconstruction. It has erected all over again the post offices with which we are plentifully supplied, the banks long in operation among us, and the apartments and college halls we already possess.

Farther south than Mexico, Brazil shows what a busy nation may be driven to. Modernism seems to have been sparked years ago by a visit by Le Corbusier. Oscar Niemeyer has tackled about the biggest task to fall to his profession in this century: laying out an entire capital, named Brasilia. There had to be new palaces for the government and the president, a hotel, a church, innumerable office buildings and apartments. Niemeyer, born in 1907 in a well-to-do family, began his work with Lucio Costa. One of his first big jobs was the celebrated Ministry of Education building in Rio de Janeiro, an early effort to coordinate all the arts.

The best architecture from the past has seemed to us everlasting. It was rooted, unshakeable, heavy as rock itself, and often rock in fact. The modernist prefers something light and more insubstantial. We do not think of the modern work as eternal, though relatively it may be. Instead, we regard it as floating, more a part of air and sky than earth. The modern builds with as little as he can, in contrast to the ancients who built with as much as they had to.

The younger Saarinen, Eero, joined those who broke away from the International Style and contributed to the freer, airy look of a lot of modern work. Like Aalto, he was a Finn and son of a man of the same profession, Eliel. When the father won second prize and $20,000 for his entry in the Chicago Tribune Tower competition, the money transferred him and his family to these shores. Like Wright, he set up his own quarters, Cranbrook Academy. Unlike Wright and more like our southern neighbors, he welcomed the assistance of allied artists, in particular the sculpture of Carl Milles. Le Corbusier, lecturing at Cranbrook, was shocked when Saarinen asked him what place he left to art. The Frenchman left none; Saarinen relied generously on it.

The son Eero had studied sculpture, his mother's calling. He changed from it to architecture and from a Paris studio to a Yale classroom. Perhaps the early training helped wean him from the cold severity of Mies. About fifteen years ago, he won a competition for a triumphal gateway in the Jefferson National Expansion Memorial in St. Louis. The telegram announcing the jury's decision was addressed merely to Saarinen. Until they opened and read it, both son and father assumed the prize went to Saarinen senior. Now going up, the completed arch will be, at six hundred and thirty feet, the tallest monument in the country. Nine hundred tons of steel will encase countless cubic yards of cement.

Saarinen the younger is responsible for the new United States embassy in London. One of his finer works is the Trans World Airlines terminal at Kennedy International Airport in New York; one of his finest the Dulles International Airport in Washington, D.C. He conceived it boldly as a sort of abstract sculpture of plane, flight, twentieth century, and the space age. Like the St. Louis arch, it is another gateway, and a worthy one, to the national capital. Sixty different airlines were to use its facilities, requiring sixty different entrances to the field. That seemed to mean a practically endless frontage. Saarinen suggested a mobile lounge or bus to taxi passengers en masse from a principal entrance to their planes. To help sell the idea to the companies, his friend the architect Charles Eames made a motion picture to show how it would work.

One spectacular performance of Eero Saarinen's was the Ingalls Hockey Rink at Yale. It is a huge dinosaur in concrete. The skeleton consists of three concrete courses. A massive backbone arches up and down, suggesting the swooping flight of a skater, and two concrete bases lie at ground level at the sides. Cables connect them, and the intervening space is roofed as if by canvas stretched taut from a tent pole. Its wide clean areas are broken only by openings for ventilation. With entrances on the ends and in the middle, it doubles as a theater in the summer. The central concrete runner lifts up again in front like the snout of a dinosaur but ends, harmlessly, in a bracket for lamps. The over-all shape imposed arbitrarily reminds us of Mies's multi-purpose structures. Neither the rink nor the temporary stage fits the interior. What was required was an open, clear space, which Saarinen provided. Does it matter that a few corners and pockets refuse to fill up with anything practical? It does not fit anything outside too well, either. Nothing in the neighborhood harmonizes with it.

This is a major problem in New Haven: the land of ivy-covered walls, battlemented towers, Doric, Ionic, and Corinthian pillars, collegiate Gothic, miniature domes, and romantic arches. Nothing jibes with anything else. The columns and gate at a cemetery hail straight from the banks of the Nile or from a stage set for *Aïda*. It is an absurd hodge-podge. At once we helplessly assume it is all beyond redemption. Nothing anyone would want to build could endure the company of anything already there.

Other college towns have to face the same situation. In New Haven, the decision was boldly taken to let Saarinen rub elbows with Colonial, Gordon Bunshaft with Renaissance, the ultra-modern with the ultra-conservative. After all, a good building is a good building in any environment. Seagram is still a marvel despite the shadow of Pan Am. The Brooklyn Bridge loses nothing by its proximity to lesser bridges. Proper siting is a great help, as we noticed in Garches. The Arc de Triomphe benefits from the Champs-Elysées; the Sainte Chapelle is the worse off for the dingy surrounding walls. The Pontalba apartments, massive twin buildings that are among the first apartments in America, of red brick, with cast-iron balcony railings, are lucky to front on the lovely square in New Orleans. But arch, chapel, and apartments are

masterpieces by themselves. If the Ingalls Rink is a masterpiece at all, it is a masterpiece where it stands. We should
not deprive ourselves of the grand adventure of living in the
new and with the new just because some old-timers built for
their age not ours.

Kahn's art gallery is a case in point. In spite of its tight
squeeze on a busy corner in New Haven, it is a treasure as is.
Louis I. Kahn's father was a stained-glass worker and one-
time soldier of the Czar, and his mother a harpist. He was
born in 1901 on an island in the Baltic Sea. His parents
brought him to this country at four to begin his American
life in poverty in Philadelphia. The ambitious boy longed for
a career as a pianist and then as a painter. He loved Philadelphia—where Louis Sullivan found an architect he was
happy to work for. Kahn found one, too: Paul P. Cret, head
of the School of Architecture at the University of Pennsylvania. Cret was no revolutionary—nor is Kahn. One of the
teacher's buildings was the Folger Shakespeare Library in
Washington. Kahn was graduated in 1924. Employed in the
city architect's office, he had charge of design for the Philadelphia Sesquicentennial of 1926. In Europe in 1928, the
moderns failed to impress him, but he was fascinated by the
ancients. Paestum in the grandeur of its ruins was his ideal
city.

He was not irrevocably committed to the old, and some
new rubbed off on him and stuck. A friend was George
Howe of Howe & Lescaze, to be remembered for their Philadelphia Saving Fund Society skyscraper, the city's first major
modern work. Howe was the financial backer of a magazine
Kahn contributed to. A sentence in one article betrayed the
incipient modernist: "We must learn how a steamboat is to
be given its character, or how a New York business building

is seen with an absolute detachment and devotion equal to
that awakened by a cathedral."

Though the depression stranded him more than once on
relief rolls, Kahn kept on doggedly building buildings. He
made the acquaintance of R. Buckminster Fuller, who is a
real revolutionary. He was employed on the Philadelphia
Psychiatric Hospital. A year at the American Academy in
Rome was followed by appointment to the Yale faculty and
the commission for the new Art Gallery. In principle, it resembles the Goodwin-Stone museum in New York: a loft
with the maximum open space, bunching stairs, elevators
and other equipment in a central core. Frame and floors
were concrete poured in place. Each floor rests on the points
of a deep network of four-sided forms, or tetrahedrons. Left
uncovered, they are the ceiling. Wires and pipes run through
the open spaces. Lights are tucked in there, too, where they
are easy to get at. There is no attempt at concealment. The
walls and columns are concrete straight out of the molds.
Partitions are movable. The entrance is in slate and glass.

Street walls are plain and bare. A section of darker brick
contributes to a harmonious integration into the adjacent old
gallery. To show off against the flat, unadorned surfaces,
Kahn, like Johnson, plants an angular oak with spindly,
spiky leaves. The somewhat crowded garden preserves a far-
branching deciduous tree and contains sculpture by Maillol,
Henry Moore, and Dimitri Hadzi.

If the main forms impress us, the details intrigue us. They
are fun, they are witty. The stairs are circular, but the railing
is in contrasting straight sections. The screen between the
uprights is rectangular—that is, standardized—and leaves
neat, open, slim triangles at top and bottom. Along the garden steps, the railing is without a screen and leans inward to

keep an unwary person's feet away from the ends where they could slip off. Garden benches are thick wood slabs. A wall consists of weathered wood slats. Ivy climbs over red bricks. Pots for flowers or shrubs are concrete and designed for use singly or in rows.

On another commission, the Richards Medical Laboratories at the University of Pennsylvania, Kahn made the most efficient use yet of precast concrete. Towers enclose stairs and air conditioning. The floors, supported on each edge by a pair of columns, are wide and free as was required.

As Johnson and Wright designed for a fair and a park, Kahn did a pleasure barge to sail on the Thames. The American Wind Symphony of Pittsburgh coasted up and down the river one summer and played water music and other music to Londoners.

If the young generation does not turn to Kahn as its mentor, then it may consider Fuller. A native New Englander, he spent the usual busy boyhood. He put together toy planes. During his summers among Maine fishermen, he says he was introduced to such "tension systems as seines, trawls, weirs, scallop drags, lobster-pot heads, and traps." He got experience in "net weaving, tieing, and splicing." That one of the oldest occupations in the world should lead to the newest and most revolutionary constructions is one of the strangest ironies.

He went to Harvard. In fact, he went twice. Each time the university discouraged his continuance for his mind seemed stubbornly fixed on other matters. If he did not deliberately follow Johnson's advice to quit school, it worked out the same way in the end. But if he was denied a degree, he was nonetheless superlatively self-educated. He had several jobs, some allied with the concrete industry. Building was his

preoccupation. One of his criteria was "maximum performance per pound of metal invested." In sober truth, steel and
aluminum were stronger for him, or acted it, then ever before for anybody.

He has taught us how to handle materials in more efficient
ways. He summons up their maximum strength, the strength
that runs with the grain. Try to break a pencil in two; it is
easy. Try to pull it in two, and we cannot. Fuller shifts his
materials around to bring them into play the strong way
rather than the weak, lengthwise instead of edgewise, to
benefit from the pull rather than take a chance on the break.
He, too, uses a system of building blocks, but space-age
blocks a world away from Fröbel's. The tensegrity mast—his
word—illustrates this. On exhibit in the Museum of Modern
Art, it is six feet tall. Based on Fuller's principles, it is, however, credited to Kenneth Snelson. Weight is transmitted
along wires. They pass through occasional tubes to separate
them and keep them in their proper functional channels. It
looks like, but it is not like, a wrecker's scaffolding. It weighs
ten pounds; it will hold six hundred pounds—"maximum
performance per pound of metal invested" marvelously demonstrated.

From the start, the housing problem worried Fuller, or he
worried it. What concerned him was not a house for a
couple, for slum dwellers, for an entire brand-new town, but
housing for millions, for all the world. He was more social-
minded and liberal than Mies and Wright—to whom such
terms do not rightly apply—and more than Le Corbusier. A
people at war, he believed, could do anything they determined to but appeared to stop thinking and achieving in
peacetime.

If cars could be mass-produced, why not houses? One
project was a ten- or twelve-story apartment weighing forty-

five tons. Hundreds or thousands could be made, he figured, for $23,000 apiece. A dirigible would hook onto one, hover over the intended site, drop an explosive to blast out a foundation, lower the apartment, and tie it in with cables and cement it there. This may sound improbable but, in fact, he did much the same thing with his smaller Dymaxion house—from his combination of the words dynamic, maximum, and ion. Helicopters pick it up and deliver it to the site.

However fascinating these ideas are to toy with in a laboratory, it took Fuller years to interest industry. In 1953, the Ford Motor Company had a problem that apparently only one man in the world could solve: R. Buckminster Fuller. It needed a ninety-three-foot dome on the Rotunda Building. In steel, it would weigh one hundred and sixty tons and crush the walls. Fuller erected an eight-and-a-half-ton dome. Part of its secret was that no extra weight was wasted to prevent the spread of the supporting walls. His dome by itself absorbed the lateral thrust. Some record was set, at least until recently, by two clear spans for the Union Tank Carbide Company in Baton Rouge, Louisiana, and Wood River, Illinois. They cover two and a half acres, have a diameter of three hundred eighty-four feet, and stand twelve stories high.

In 1954, the United States Marine Corps cried help. It stocked forty-seven different types of shelter, which for their construction required two thousand nine hundred items such as nails, screws, hammers, and all sorts and sizes of materials and tools. Fuller devised a paper-board container for six men. It measured fourteen feet through. Since the occupants discarded it when they had finished with it, it earned the name of the "Kleenex house." It was not gossamer, it would not tuck into the pocket of fatigue clothes, but it could be stored away in one of its own closets—if Fuller built a closet into it. It was merely a rigid framework with a flexible cover.

The Marines reported jubilantly that it "required only four percent of the weight of the former solutions, six percent of the packaged volume, fourteen percent of the cost and less than one percent of the erection man hours." Comparable huts with fiberglas domes were set up on our Arctic DEW line across Canada.

Fuller has proposed a two-mile-wide dome to seal off midtown New York. Weighing eighty thousand tons, it would be assembled in five-ton sections set in place by helicopters. This coverall would save, he argues, the incalculable expenses of air conditioning, street cleaning, snow removal, head colds, umbrellas, rubbers, and so on.

One of his practical works is the Climatron—again presumably a name he made up. It rises like the first puff of a monster bubble in Shaw's Garden in St. Louis, Missouri. It has a one-hundred-seventy-foot diameter and is seventy feet high. It is an enormous greenhouse. Architecturally and scientifically, it is more important than Joseph Paxton's famous greenhouse-style Crystal Palace. The plan was developed by Dr. Frits W. Went and local architects according to Fuller's principles. Officials describe it as a geodesic dome made of aluminum tubing in hexagonal patterns. Attached to the interior face of the two-layer dome is a sheet of transparent Plexiglas a quarter of an inch thick. The support, that is, is outside; the actual covering inside. The over-all weight is shunted down along five lunes or ribs to five piers. The ground surface covered thus is a little more than half an acre. The construction suggests a giant umbrella. Or a little over half an orange with an end sliced off stands on the exposed surface. It is wonderfully suited to its purpose. Several levels are arranged inside. Two air conditioners maintain the temperature of a tropical or semitropical jungle. There are more than a thousand kinds of plants growing in it.

Fuller bubbles over with ideas. A pressure gun gives him a good bath—he says—with only a gallon of water; in a world where water grows scarcer, this is not idle invention. His principal contribution is his structures, closer to pure functionalism than architecture has ever come. He is a teacher and lives under one of his own domes. The space is not devised for the occupant's convenience; he fits himself to it. But it should be no harder to adapt oneself and one's belongings to a curved wall or one with frequent bends than to a flat one. The constructions are in their way handsome, perhaps handsomer than the boxes that monotonously line our streets. They belong on no known landscape unless it is the landscape of the moon. An ancient Italian community consists of beehive houses. If they can draw tourists, why wouldn't Fuller's round tops draw customers? Their cost is incredibly low—and almost a fifth of our people lives in slums.

High Spots

The types of buildings to which the architect turns his hand
—and turns it eagerly, for he thrives on problems, and the
tougher and more unusual the better—run from A for airport to Z for zoo. In between are warehouses, railroad stations, bus terminals, planetariums, greenhouses, stadiums,
hangars, churches, synagogues, homes, schools, studios, mu-
seums, halls, banks, apartments, offices, memorials, bridges,
theaters, barges, pavilions, hotels, restaurants, dormitories,
rinks.

Wherever you travel, to Latin America, Europe, Asia,
Russia, north and south, and all across the United States,
you encounter examples of the modern. It is easy to identify.

If it rises fifteen or twenty stories or higher, then it is probably new. It is characterized by ribbon windows, plain walls, concrete surfaces, *pilotis,* and cantilevered porches, roofs, and floors. We can build skyscrapers twice and three times as high as before. We can bridge chasms that had always defied us. We can enclose the biggest spaces ever.

The world is fortunate, too, in a great abundance of architectural talent. No mere listing is an adequate acknowledgment of the outstanding work of André Lurçat in France, Masachika Murata in Japan, and Robert H. Matthew for, specially, the Royal Festival Hall in London. At home, Lincoln Center alone has Max Abramovitz's Philharmonic Hall and Pietro Belluschi's Juilliard School. Sarasota, Florida, has a Sarasota high school and airport buildings by Paul Rudolph. Denver boasts of I. M. Pei's Mile High Center, New York has Pei's Kips Bay Plaza Apartments, and the campus of Harvard University will be the site of the John F. Kennedy Memorial Library, to be designed by Pei. Minoru Yamasaki, painter and teacher as well as architect, has buildings in St. Louis, Cleveland, Minneapolis, Seattle, and of course Detroit—in particular, the McGregor Memorial Conference Center of Wayne State University there.

Some of the rare achievements, among them in particular a few churches, schools, and bridges, deserve special visits. The most exciting form is undoubtedly the bridge. We discover it first as children. We build one when we lay a board across the stones in a brook. The Verrazano-Narrows Bridge is not much different except that the board and stones are bigger and the brook deeper.

Part of the lasting fascination exercised by the bridge lies in the element of danger. One that was half finished fell into the St. Lawrence River. Another broke to pieces above the

Tacoma Narrows. Thornton Wilder wrote a book that succeeded about a bridge that failed: *The Bridge of San Luis Rey*. We all remember the song about London Bridge falling down. According to a saying, a dogtrot of the right calamitous rhythm will set up in a bridge the shivers and shakes that mean ruination—though no dog has ever been caught in the act.

Besides the perverse attraction of risk, bridges automatically draw crowds. When travelers must cross a river, they congregate at the only crossing place. They meet, they talk, they exchange news, they hold revels—as they once danced on the bridge at Avignon. They build shops along the parapets. Whether we call it the new bridge or the old, the Pont Neuf in Paris did its brisk business and so did the Ponte Vecchio over the Arno in Florence.

Man aware of his insignificance is reminded by the sight of his handiwork that he has had his exalted moments. We go to a bridge to cross it and also to marvel, whether it is the Golden Gate Bridge, the Brooklyn, the Firth of Forth, or the Eads. One ancient glory is the Pont du Gard, the huge three-tiered aqueduct near Nîmes in southern France. The Romans erected it nearly two thousand years ago. They were ignorant of International Style, "less is more," and "form follows function." Yet they religiously practiced what the modernist preaches. They could not have done with a single stone less; they strived consciously not to pile on a single extra one. French engineers in running a roadway across the Gard River in this century backed it up against the aqueduct to benefit by its enduring strength.

The maker of perhaps our most beautiful bridges is the Swiss Robert Maillart. He molds them, you would swear, out of something more malleable than reinforced concrete. They have the elegance and delicacy a sculptor's fingers impart to clay. They soar, they almost fly, they wind over a deep abyss for a railroad track or a highway. They look so fragile that officialdom wrangled with Maillart over every early project. Yet there they remain as light as the Alps are ponderous and to some people as persuasive a reason for traveling in Switzerland as the Alps themselves.

The structure of a bridge, whether cantilever, suspension, arch, or a combination, is likely to be imposed by the terrain, the required length, the height of the banks, the nature of the soil, the availability of material. Or it may be a causeway over shallow water as over Lake Pontchartrain in Louisiana. If the material is stone, the quarry gets an accurate drawing of every single stone. If it is metal, drawings for every separate piece go to the mill or foundry. Meanwhile, the designs are traced full size on some floor big enough in a place called the template loft. The templates, thin wood or metal, are shaped with absolute exactness. The spot for every rivet and bolt is marked. Templates and castings or steel are brought together at the work site, the markings are transferred, and the builders take over.

The bigger the job, the more elaborate the process. The most elaborate process of all has been in the news the last few years: the Verrazano-Narrows Bridge. With all its decks open, it can carry forty-eight million cars a year, or approximately one hundred and thirty thousand a day or six thousand an hour. It cost nearly a third of a billion dollars. Its purpose was to divert from jam-packed New York City the north-south through traffic between New England, New Jersey, and more distant points.

There never was a bridge like it. The roadways hang more than two hundred feet above the water, allowing plenty of headway for thirteen thousand ships a year to sail under it. The two towers weigh twenty-seven thousand tons apiece and are nearly seven hundred feet tall. Because of their height, the distance separating them, and the curvature of the earth's surface, they tip apart an inch or two at the top. The suspension cables were spun out of a hundred and forty thousand miles of wire. Road sections of almost four hundred tons each were put together in an assembly yard on the Jersey shore and floated on barges to the site. At the elevation of the first one, the monster cables sagged twenty inches. More computers were needed to figure how to adjust the other sections to the necessary split-hair levels.

The designer was Othmar H. Ammann, a native of Switzerland, the land of Le Corbusier and Maillart. For a long time, he was director of engineering for the Port of New York Authority and chief engineer of the Triborough Bridge Authority. He retired at sixty, not to quit work but rather to start, for he organized the firm of Ammann & Whitney. Suspension bridges have been his specialty. The George Washington Bridge and the Golden Gate in San Francisco show his hand. The Narrows job boasts the longest suspension span ever: four thousand two hundred and sixty feet. This means a passage in the empty air of four-fifths of a mile.

A bridge is subjected to very special strains. In addition to its own dead weight, it must support live weight that varies with the traffic; the impact, caused by the speed of traffic; temperature changes; wind pressure. At the Firth of Forth in Scotland, one-thousand-seven-hundred-foot spans extend from the towers by cantilever. As an indication of the magnitude of subsidiary engineering problems, about half the steel in these cantilevers bears the dead weight and traffic. Almost as much more, or roughly the other half, is required merely to stiffen it against the wind. Lack of this stiffener brought down the Tacoma Narrows Bridge. Erected at the cost of almost fifty million dollars, it had suspension spans of record length. Four months after it opened in 1940, a fitful gale—not the rhythmic dogtrot—set up disastrous oscillations that tore it apart.

From a bridge to a library seems a long jump, but this particular one is a sort of suspension library. Four corner posts of granite hold it in the air. They are not Le Corbusier's *pilotis* but isolated bases like the five for the ribs at Fuller's Climatron. It is the Beinecke Rare Book and Manuscript Library, another brave Yale venture. The work of Skidmore, Owings & Merrill, it was the particular concern of Gordon Bunshaft.

It is a shell and then the meat, or a jewel box and the jewel. The jewel is the stack of rare books, standing free of the container, rising sixty feet, with an all-over glass skin. Illumination is entirely artificial. Since there was not enough of the onyx that Bunshaft favored for the shell, he settled for Vermont marble panels one and a quarter inches thick. Daylight penetrates faintly. The whole area between shell and content, including the lounge, acts as an antichamber. It has a cloistered, sequestered atmosphere. Most of the working space lies underground. A tunnel under High Street connects it with the Sterling Library. The structure confronts a sunken court decorated with sculpture by Isamu Noguchi. Besides cabalistic markings on the floor, there are three shapes: a pyramid for time, a circle for the sun, and a cube for chance —the cube that to the Russians meant purity and to Frank Lloyd Wright Fascism. This white marble assemblage, Noguchi says, "is intended to invoke a dramatic landscape. . . . The landscape is purely that of the imagination, it is nowhere, yet somehow familiar."

From in front, the part above ground has a serene coffered or waffled surface. It looks like a great white square cake or a chest on four squat legs. No doors or windows show. Lights are sunk in the ceiling above the plaza. There are a couple of rows of benches—and thousands of visitors.

A church in nearby Stamford has attracted wide attention. Most parishioners now cherish it as a true place of worship. The outside observer may feel some reservations. It is the First Presbyterian Church designed by Wallace K. Harrison of Rockefeller Center and United Nations fame. It is half a block long and six stories high. Harrison boldly employs a new symbol. Many churches are laid out on the plan of a cross flat on the ground. This is based on another sign of Christ: the fish. The fish is upright; it is the upper half mounted, as it were, on a board as a trophy. The outline shows the rise and fall of the back, the dip, and the broadened tail. It is intended to have, and has, a recognizable fish profile. The curve would parallel roughly that of Saarinen's hockey rink.

One hundred and fifty-two precast concrete forms, triangles or quadrangles, solid or skeletal, constitute the frame and walls of the sanctuary. Some over three stories high weigh eleven tons. They tilt inward at about a seventy-five-degree angle. The handsome red, blue, and green glass came from a French studio. The Crucifixion and Resurrection are suggested by some twenty thousand inch-thick pieces. Mahogany pews seat seven hundred. The chancel contains a thirty-two-foot cross. A sounding board in the shape of an open Bible is braced above the pulpit. A stone from Wartburg, significant in the Martin Luther story, and another from a Scottish island with Presbyterian associations are buried in the floor. The acoustics are excellent. Outside, overlapping slate simulates fish scales. An abstract sculpture representing Christ on the cross rises above the main entrance. The same spindly oaks that Kahn planted around the New Haven gallery grow in the yard.

This is a prestige church, as it says. It is probably the largest and wealthiest Protestant church in Stamford. On the whole, it oddly reverses the usual scheme: the building is representational, the appurtenances abstract. Originally occupying a conventional structure with red carpeting and a gloomy interior, the church had planned to build in the same style. When Harrison, an Episcopalian, offered several designs, the fish shape was approved. There is more color here, inside and outside, than at Rockefeller Center and United Nations put together. If older members of the congregation felt a little ill at ease, the younger people enjoyed their spiritual home and took pride in it.

The city for which the name Saarinen may be best remembered, and the city with a pair of the finest churches in the country hardly a mile apart, is Columbus, Indiana. This county seat is very lucky to number among its residents a manufacturer who busies himself with the beautification of his community. When the school board chooses an architect approved by his company, the company pays his fee. Good architecture is wonderful in itself, but when it does not come out of taxes, it is more wonderful.

About a quarter century ago Saarinen senior was called in for the First Christian Church commission—the manufacturer's son studied at the Saarinens' Cranbrook as young Kaufmann studied at Wright's Taliesin. Saarinen, with his son Eero as an occasional assistant, built a blond and white edifice reached by shallow steps. In the paneled front, the main door and, directly above, a plain cross are set just off center. A separate brick tower rises near the entrance—reminder of San Gimignano in Italy—and balances it neatly. Reduced in size, it is handsomely and sensitively repeated near the side entrance. Many activities can be accommodated in several auditoriums, a kitchen, reception rooms, Sunday School quarters, and gymnasium.

Easily the most remarkable sight in this fortunate city is the second church designed by Eero alone. The plans were finished only weeks before his death. It is the North Christian Church. This comparatively young congregation acquired its first home under the leadership of its first full-time minister, Dr. James L. Stoner. The church committee interviewed twelve leading architects before selecting Saarinen.

We descend a couple of steps—as at Johnson's New York State Fair pavilion—to enter the building proper, a hexagonal on a platform of earth and concrete. A slender two-hundred-foot spire surmounts it. A Dutch-cast bell rings at its base, and a five-foot cross crowns it. The initial fund raised was $300,000. The final cost, a secretary confesses with a shake of her head, was one million dollars. The result cannot be measured in dollars and cents, not even in thousands of dollars. The building in its sunken plaza amounts to religion in the round. It is a sort of pagoda. The hexagonal construction shows plainly. It is meant to, as in the crisscross of beams in the basement ceiling. This is the service area. The baptistry, also six-sided, and offices and other administrative quarters occupy the first or main floor. The sanctuary is the equivalent of a mezzanine. It is one of the few truly lovely, spiritual church interiors of our time—a time, architects have regretted, not conducive to church building. The religious mood makes itself felt overpoweringly. It is worked with superb artistry into the shapes, the colors, the materials. The wood is dark. The pulpit stands handsomely before banked organ pipes. The ceiling is subdued silver. It has one fault noted in other places: the many gray concrete step edges are not marked. If some parishioner does not miss his footing occasionally, it is a near miracle.

The splendid pristine condition of this church reminds us that some occupants, religious and secular, itch to "improve," as they suppose, the work of their betters. They prefer their own interior. There seem to be no changes in the Saarinens'. But some good worshipers have altered distressingly a church in Mexico, D.F., by Felix Candela. They hope to be regarded as their parish's well wishers. They have acted more like vandals. It is the Church of Our Lady of the Miraculous Medal. Like Saarinen senior, Candela erected a separate tower, slender and openwork, with a symbolic star at its peak. Three charming primitive chandeliers light the nave. Pillars that drop down from the solid, overhanging walls—slanted inward like Harrison's in Stamford—twist and thin out into slight shapely shafts.

Completed in 1956, the church promptly published a brochure with photos and description: "Behind the altar rises an expanse of brick wall. . . . Into that wall is set the altarpiece, consisting of only three figures: in the center the Virgin, an angel on either side. . . . As a setting for worship it is spectacular in its purity and simplicity." So it was indeed. Since then the purity and simplicity have vanished because people demanded something common and ordinary. They felt ill at ease with plain, bare, overpowering beauty. So they doctored it, pottered with it, ruined it. The red bricks disappeared behind a fussy blue hanging with a frilly border. The sculpture by Antonio Ballester is still romantic and handsome, but the entire grand effect has been badly harmed.

A better Candela still not tampered with stands on the outskirts of Cuernavaca. This is a chapel on a hillside above the resort town. It is merely a shell, in effect, half a cornucopia. The altar is placed at the small end before a glass wall. Through it the panorama of valley and city spreads out before the worshipers. The opening is a hundred feet wide.

The roof soars seventy feet high over a bank of low concrete benches. It is shelter but not an enclosure. What if it rains? In this climate, it apparently does not rain at the hour of service. Beside the entrance rises a separate tower in the form of a great cross. Small openings dot its several faces every few yards. It is a dovecote. The birds of peace fly constantly in and out.

In England at Coventry, the wartime bombing of St. Michael's Cathedral required its replacement. Sir Basil Spence, who was in charge, decreed, "The new cathedral should grow from the old and be incomplete without it." A lofty porch links the awesome ruins with the modern structure. The walls, solid, pink-gray sandstone, rest on nearly seven hundred piles driven down twenty or thirty feet to rock. The interior is finished in plaster with acoustic properties. The floor is a concrete slab. The walls are sawtoothed. Besides giving added strength, this angled construction provides spaces for thin vertical panels of beautiful stained glass. Sir Basil called on England's best artists for help. Graham Sutherland designed the immense tapestry behind the altar. John Piper was responsible for the windows. Sir Jacob Epstein sculptured the twenty-five-foot bronze of a triumphant St. Michael and a fallen devil braced dramatically outside near the porch.

All across our country, new churches spring up. Ministers and their flocks appear open-minded about modernity. They are much less conservative than most businesses, professional firms, individual home builders and buyers, and almost all real-estate developers. One fine serious rival challenges them, however: the schools. Teachers are sensitive about their times and aware of progress. School boards hate to squander an unnecessary penny. More consolidations mean fewer buildings. One is always cheaper to put up than two. Furthermore, the plain fashion of modernism is by itself less expensive than the ornate old—the little red schoolhouse costs more per cubic foot than International Style.

Except for the home, the school is the most familiar building. It has become as streamlined as the auto. Some faultfinders say that just as public parks are being opened in the country where there are no people, schools are established in the country where there are no pupils. They are centrally located, however, for the benefit of several participating communities. Outlying land is cheaper. Bus service is furnished anyway. Larger schools permit a greater variety of subjects and higher teacher salaries. Changes in educational methods account for some physical changes, but architectural advances account for most of them.

Richard J. Neutra, Eliel Saarinen, and William Lescaze rank with the best men in this field; particularly noteworthy is Neutra's Corona School in Bell, California, an early one-story building pioneering in the use of sliding doors to run inside and outside together. In general, the new schools look somewhat alike. A lot of land surrounds them, and faculty cars and buses are parked on a concrete plaza. They are usually one-story high, never more than two. The walls are mostly glass. Rooms are arranged by several basic plans. Sometimes pavilions reach out from a central administrative core, star-fashion. Or classrooms are spaced along each side of a corridor. Or they bunch around an open play area. Separate buildings shelter different activities in college-campus style.

How does a town go about getting a new school? Joseph Bernard, principal of the Greater Gallitzin Joint Junior-Senior High School, in Gallitzin, Pennsylvania, describes the process he recently followed, and it is typical. The old building was crowded and needed repairs. Remodeling would cost $700,000, the brand-new job $1,266,000. Enrollment was estimated on a ten-year basis. State authorities, informed of the figure, prescribed the number of rooms. Architects were asked to submit bids.

The town owned thirty acres on a hilltop. Winter brought wind and snow, but the summits of the Allegheny Mountains were the grand scenery. The chief material is cement blocks. Everything is located on one floor. Bernard much prefers this to his former three-story quarters. The auditorium doubles as a gym. Folding bleachers seat seven hundred, or more than the population of the school, and there is space for chairs for five hundred more. The kitchen has expensive modern equipment. The stage would be the envy of some off-Broadway companies in New York. Lights are fluorescent. The art room has its own kiln, the shop fine new machines, the library a growing stock of books and its own librarian.

Some young people may not be mature enough to benefit from high school. Yet if they can enter a place like this, they undergo an urbanizing influence. If they don't get something out of the class, they may get something out of the classroom —clean, bright, freshly furnished, implying sophistication. The new school offers something never available in the little red schoolhouse. If the little red schoolhouse offered something not available here, it is not architecture's concern.

15 | City Planning

If it was hard to imagine a walk in a landscape that had disappeared, in some ways the actual walk in the present is harder. Our cities are bad walking places. People and autos slow us down or stop us. We move around best by riding. Bicycling on many streets is dangerous and on most sidewalks is forbidden. The auto alone remains. But in some places at some hours, riding is no faster than walking. To fly to a distant city may take an hour, or as long as to drive to the airport. That is, you travel two hundred fifty miles by air in the time required for twenty-five by car—like the Harrison and Le Corbusier elevators, ten times as fast in one as in the other.

168

Circulation is a key aspect of architecture. The architect of your house should first make it a good one. Then he must bear in mind that it ought to be accessible in surroundings protected against deterioration. Many of your fathers, certainly your grandfathers, spent ten minutes in the morning and ten at night on a healthy and enjoyable walk to work. Now millions of Americans, Englishmen, and Frenchmen, too, get up an hour or an hour and a half early to drive to the suburban station, park, board the commuter train, and transfer to bus or taxi for the last lap to the office. They progress from smoky waiting room to unaired coach and smelly bus. There cannot be a single American city in which it is possible to drive a mile as fast as could be done five years ago. Five years ago the same statement would have been just as accurate.

Build your home at the North Pole, the Equator, on a mountain summit, you still have to get there. Traffic seems to a city to be a proof of progress. Does it build miles of high-speed roads to see them deserted? Traffic commissioners rush around cutting down every tree, shoving sidewalks back against doorways, and presenting the extra space to the autoist. That may get the first few cars there faster for the first few months, but no more. A city block lined with two-story houses provides room for everyone to park at the curb and move up and down in the middle. Erect an apartment on the corner, that is, quarters for twenty families instead of two, and the squeeze begins. Replace all the houses with apartments, and no room is left to park or move. This has happened in hundreds of cities and keeps on happening. The trimming and the crowding deprive your precious corner of the world of shade and of a livable, residential quality. You are all the more impatient to hop into the car and drive all the faster to get away from the home you ought to love, from the apartment that has turned into a hive, and the street that has turned into a warren.

The traffic commissioner's opposite in the countryside is the highway engineer. He, too, is keen on cutting down trees. His grand superhighway can run across only a level, barren landscape. He is encouraged by the real-estate developer, who feels some special hatred for trees and slashes them down right and left. Many of us are victims of that ugly blight, the suburban sprawl. Houses inch out one by one along miles of road one deep on each side, wasting the vast hinterland. It means a little lawn around a little house too crowded by its neighbors on a street with too much traffic, too few trees, and too high utility costs.

Many city planning commissions do little more than rubber-stamp the questionable propositions of "realtors" greedy for a fast buck. The New York zoning law might as well be erased from the books. If the Pan Am Building is a monstrous midtown disaster, nothing in the law prevented it from being three times as monstrous. The lot is worth forty-five million dollars. Have we the right to deny the owner, man or corporation, a full return on his property? Has he the right to build a bottleneck plumb in the middle of our city? We interfere regularly in individual affairs for the general good. We conscript a man for the Army. We condemn property for a public purpose. Could we go a bit further? Could we close some streets to autos?

Le Corbusier said architecture included everything. One hundred fifty years before that, another Frenchman declared, "There is not a man on earth who cannot be helped in some way by an architect." Lewis Mumford argues that no one can build a house properly unless he controls the space around it. Frank Lloyd Wright said everyone should have an acre to live on. As he figured it, Texas had enough acres for all, with the rest of the country no doubt abandoned to farming or vacationing or the Indians.

City planning courses have been offered in some universities for several years. It may take a lifetime to learn, but we can always make a start. Without some effort, our cities will be not merely ugly but strangled.

Two things helped cause this condition: the skyscraper and the auto—and we are proud of them both. We are gregarious. We like company. We enjoy living like birds and animals in flocks and herds. Large numbers provide advantages beyond the reach of villagers: theater, museum, concert hall, and sports arena. Then we carry the process too far. We are to blame not for what we started but for what we do not stop. Universal urban forces shove us around. A man who owns a house collects rent from one family. With an apartment, he collects twenty times as much. Before long the tax assessor values his property so high he can pay the bill only by renting to twenty families. So he crowds and inconveniences you and me all the more, or the tax assessor does, or the general metropolitan situation does.

Since a city has no faults that man did not give it, he can remedy what is wrong if he has a mind to. The Greeks who worshiped proportion and mistrusted gigantism lopped off a big section of an oversize community and sent it away to found a colony. In our time, many solutions have been suggested and a few realized. Tomorrow's architect may perform no more valuable or welcome service than to let us live together in reasonable numbers, not too close to neighbors, yet close enough. As his second contribution to our future, he would open up traffic arteries so we can breathe again.

Sometimes the fine urban approach just happens as with the Villa Stein in Garches. Most architects would rather work on an entire city than one meager building. Wright's

Broadacre City was four square miles. Other suggestions were the City in Space, Citta Nuova, Cité Moderne. Le Corbusier designed Radiant City. They had their predecessors. Residents of an island in Venice go afoot on minor errands and by boat on speedier, more important ones. One does not impede the other. Christopher Wren would have rebuilt London after the great fire of 1666. Major Charles Pierre L'Enfant of the French engineers was borrowed by our government to lay out the city of Washington. Just over a hundred and fifty years ago, the grid plan for New York City was drawn. Hundreds of streets and avenues were fixed then and have remained frozen ever since.

England is putting up New Towns, complete units with all the necessities. To match that, we have had for over three decades Radburn, New Jersey. It is not far off the western end of the George Washington Bridge. Though the run into New York is drab, it is fairly fast. Clarence Stein and Henry Wright created the Radburn Plan.

You enter town on a reasonably fast highway. At a glance, it resembles countless ordinary small communities. One turn off the route sends you into the promised land. It is a land not of front yards but back, not of straight-edged building lots but curved, not of traffic hazards but, in effect, one huge safety zone. Secondary roads run through, but they are strictly for wheeled traffic and do not even have sidewalks. Leading from them are short, winding, inviting, dead-end drives long enough to accommodate perhaps fifteen houses set close together. They have little lawn in front—Le Corbusier had almost none. In the back lie long shady walks far from traffic. Children follow them to and from school. Here are the grass, shrubs, and trees—with no one to cut them down—that provide the country flavor all living quarters need.

New York has little green outside Central Park. In contrast, parks and playgrounds are plentiful in European cities —great expanses of them in London, Rome, and Paris. There are a lot in Mexico, too. Most small towns south of the border have fewer autos than we do. The women do not wear Fifth Avenue fashions. There are more cows, burros, horses, and horseback riders in the streets than in all the TV westerns we have seen. Even so, most of the towns boast a charming square, or perhaps two. It has a bandstand, benches, parqueted walks, a lush growth of palms and other trees, and a lot of birds. The public strolls there, sits there, relaxes there.

We must stop regarding a square as a place where we cannot put up a building for profit. No building is profitable to society in the long run unless it has a corner of a square available somewhere. Yet a greensward fifteen miles off in the country is not enough. It must be near enough to walk to. Every child is entitled to grass to lie on, and a man deserves a tree to lean his back against. In this respect, Americans are worse off than Mexicans, worse off than western Europeans. Then what does it matter if we are richer?

Hartford, Connecticut, is one of numerous cities trying to become a better place to live in. The shabbier stores and less profitable ventures of its citizens had usurped its riverfront. Now it has been transformed into a vast, bright, open plaza for pedestrians only. On several levels there are pools, occasional sculpture, planting, a handsome slab fountain, and a picturesque clock tower; also a bank, drugstore, hotel, insurance company, and TV and radio station. One building with an oval ground plan, pointed ends, and swelling middle rises boldly on eight huge piers. The entire area should benefit from summer breezes sweeping from the Connecticut River across this low-lying and sometimes muggy capital.

St. Louis, Missouri, is renovating its waterfront hand-somely. First of all, it has carefully preserved such treasures as the Eads Bridge and the Wainwright skyscraper. Notably it has restored a row of typical old waterfront houses two or three stories high, in red and white brick, as quaint as buildings lining a canal in Ghent or Bruges. The city also has cleared a wide, deep swath back into town to create a spacious esplanade in the shadow of the great Saarinen arch. Brooklyn is beautifying itself—New York City acts shame-lessly indifferent. Improvements in Philadelphia include a fine new look around Independence Hall. Pittsburgh's Golden Triangle, where the Allegheny and Monongahela Rivers form the Ohio, has been refurbished with shiny sky-scrapers and a park.

Great and welcome changes have been proposed in the nation's capital. In 1791, Major L'Enfant's plan for Wash-ington was based on focal points. Streets would radiate from government buildings and squares. The prospect was regal and picturesque but impractical in many ways. What was bad in the eighteenth century was worse in the twentieth. The avenues are too wide for pedestrians to cross with safety and ill suited to the speeding auto. Vistas were not enough. Even so, unwanted run-down buildings have turned up along once promising avenues and boulevards.

President Kennedy appointed a council of architects and planners to tell how to restore to Pennsylvania Avenue the splendor originally envisioned. The recommendations would accomplish wonders—if they were carried out. Open spaces would frame the National Gallery of Art and the Archives Building more impressively. By the White House, there would be a square as spacious as the Place de la Concorde in Paris—we seek abroad the comparisons our own country cannot provide. There would be rows of trees. Sidewalks on different levels would serve, incidentally, in place of stands for spectators at parades. Only autos on business would be admitted to the area. Through traffic would detour via a sunken road.

Washington is the show place. We descend on it in hordes at graduation time to see how the government works. We visit it for the cherry blossoms, the Lincoln Memorial, Arlington Cemetery, and many historical associations. But we live in Millville, Springtown, Maplewood, and Johnsboro. What matters immediately is what goes on right around us, up and down our street, in and out of our town.

Architecture begins at home. We are citizens and taxpayers. Let's be fighters, too. Let's hold onto our greens. If we can make the woodman spare that tree in our yard, on our street, in our park, all trees will be spared. If we can make our little corner perfect, all corners will be made perfect.

16 | Where Now?

We cannot all live in palaces. Yet what is the perfect home but a palace? In that sense, we could all be palace dwellers.

We are not that yet. Perhaps the modern architect in his first seventy-five years has done little more than get his hand in. He is beginning only now to appreciate the tremendous possibilities of steel and concrete and glass. He has built the longest bridges ever, roofed over the greatest spaces ever, and mounted into the air higher than ever before. But those are stunts. What can he do for you and me and our daily pattern of living?

He has produced a lot of gadgetry that adds to our comfort. He still has to give us, however, the perfect house. Is

Mies a little stiff? Are Wright's interiors dark and crowded? Can the man who puts so many servants' rooms into his houses be just the man we need? We know the perfect temple—the Parthenon; the perfect cathedral—Chartres; the perfect bridge—the Eads; the perfect apartment in the perfect setting—the Pontalba. What about the perfect house, the perfect approach, the perfect town?

We can define the perfect house only in general terms. It has to do with such ordinary and commonplace things that "perfect" seems pretentious or academic. It is where we leave our rubbers, where the cookie jar is, where we sit to watch TV, where our friends come to see us. Also it is the place we reach by driving through the Bois de Boulogne and the Park of St. Cloud. Also it is in the center of Radburn. It is near a Saarinen church. It faces a park.

It is all the harder to envisage the architecture of tomorrow because architects will not be alone in creating it. It will be affected by unpredictable technological advances. It has been suggested that we can some day pick up the phone, order a house, and have it delivered in hours. Maybe a dirigible will blast a hole and lower it in place. Maybe the land will be so crowded we shall build on floating islands or on flying platforms. Maybe it will be possible to blow a house as a glass blower blows a vase or pitcher. Some fantastic ideas proposed fifty years ago—apartments soaring to several hundred stories, airplanes and helicopters instead of cars to speed to work in—have yet to be realized.

Certain sections of the country are changing their character drastically. On the eastern seaboard, there used to be Boston and New York. There were smaller places in between, Springfield, New Haven, Providence. In between them came stretches of wide open country. Boston and New York now crowd close together. It is not that travel time has been reduced by planes. It is more: smaller cities and country spaces are being absorbed, or consumed. Houses crawl over more and more ground. It is probably no longer possible to ride from the Massachusetts capital to New York and ever be out of sight of a house or indeed rows of houses.

Where houses move in, the architect should move in, too. Unless we commit ourselves to his care and the care of his fellows such as the city planner, we shall have some houses with too much land, some with too little, and never the perfect house among them. We shall tie traffic up in knots. We shall do ourselves out of the playgrounds, parks, trees, and grass we need to be a happy and healthy people.

Are we astounded at what the architect has done so far? Then wait, he cries, till I really get going! We have only to define the perfect physical environment for living, determine we must have it, and work for it. Then we shall have it.

There is more than one Athens, for some communities have taken the name in the vain hope some of the substance would cling to it. There is even more than one Parthenon. A man tried to build one atop a height in Edinburgh, and it came rightly to be called his folly. We can never recapture the past. But we have a wonderful present if only we use it. There is no sight in the world like the magnificent skyline of New York, whether you view it from down the harbor or from the Jersey shore or from, say, the middle of the Queensboro Bridge. But down around the bottom of those towers there is a great need for some of the amenities, some softness and agreeableness. We can dress life grandly. We can make life efficient. Now let's try to make it more worth living. The architect who could do the big job can do all the necessary little ones if only we give him the chance.

Notes

Quotations used in this book are taken from the following sources:

Page 51: Behrendt, Walter Curt, *Modern Building: Its Nature, Problems and Forms,* New York, Harcourt, Brace & World, 1937.

Pages 54 and 60: Van Rensselaer, Mrs. Schuyler, *Henry Hobson Richardson and His Works,* Boston, Houghton Mifflin, 1888.

Page 62: Bush-Brown, Albert, *Louis Sullivan,* New York, Braziller, 1960.

Page 63: Morrison, Hugh, *Louis Sullivan: Prophet of Modern Architecture,* New York, Museum of Modern Art and W. W. Norton, 1935.

Pages 66, 67 (lines 1-4), and 157 (lines 23-24): Sullivan, Louis H., *Kindergarten Chats and Other Writings,* New York, Wittenborn, 1947.

Pages 67 (line 19), 69-70, 75, 77-78, 88 (lines 2-4 and 16-17), 91-92, 92 (lines 8-10 and 16-17), 93, and 94: Wright, Frank Lloyd, *The Future of Architecture,* New York, Horizon Press, 1953.

Pages 67 (lines 12-13, 29-30, and 31-32), 76 (lines 14 and 22-23), 79, 82, 85, 86, and 96: Farr, Finis, *Frank Lloyd Wright,* New York, Scribner, 1961.

Pages 76 (line 16), 87, and 126: Blake, Peter, *The Master Builders,* New York, Knopf, 1960.

Page 110: Le Corbusier Talks With Students, New York, Orion, 1961.

Pages 112 and 117-118: Le Corbusier, *When the Cathedrals Were White,* New York, McGraw-Hill, 1947.

Page 113: Banham, Reyner, *Theory and Design in the First Machine Age,* London, Architectural Press, 1960.

Pages 127 (lines 12 and 22), 129, 132, and 157 (line 23): Johnson, Philip C., *Mies van der Rohe,* New York, Museum of Modern Art, 1947.

Pages 138, 148-149: Scully, Vincent, Jr., *Modern Architecture,* New York, Braziller, 1961.

Pages 150, 151 (lines 1-2 and 20-21), and 153: McHale, John, *R. Buckminster Fuller,* New York, Braziller, 1962.

Page 160: Noguchi, Isamu, *Explanation of the Sculpture Garden of the Beinecke Rare Book and Manuscript Library, Yale University,* released by library, 1964.

Page 164: Iglesia de la Medalla Milagrosa, Mexico, D. F.

Page 165: The Cathedral Church of St. Michael, Coventry, Stockport, England, Cloister Press, 1962.

Page 170: Christ, Yvan, *Projets et Divagations de Claude-Nicolas Ledoux, architecte du roi,* Paris, Minotaure, 1964.

Bibliography

The walks proposed at the start of the story were not merely for the story's sake. Architecture is a physical thing, beyond the power of words or pictures to describe adequately. It has to be seen and felt and lived with and walked in and through. Since there is architecture all around us, it is easy to get invaluable first-hand experiences.

Reading is, of course, the conventional and the convenient introduction. There are the usual reference works like the *Encyclopaedia Britannica*. The best books are not general but specific. They concern the individual architect and his work. Sometimes he wrote himself; more often he has been the object of a study about him as a person and about his work. Some of these authors—among others Bush-Brown, Drexler, Farr, Hitchcock, McHale, Morrison, Scully—are even more important for being the sources of all too rare biographical information. Here are some titles:

Alazard, Jean, *Le Corbusier,* New York, Universe Books, 1959.

Brownell, Baker, and Wright, Frank Lloyd, *Architecture and Modern Life,* New York, Harper, 1937.

Bush-Brown, Albert, *Louis Sullivan,* New York, Braziller, 1960.

Christ, Yvan, *Projets et Divagations de Claude-Nicolas Ledoux, architecte du roi,* Paris, Minotaure, 1964.

Drexler, Arthur, *Ludwig Mies van der Rohe,* New York, Braziller, 1960.

Farr, Finis, *Frank Lloyd Wright,* New York, Scribner, 1961.

Hitchcock, Henry-Russell, Jr., *The Architecture of H. H. Richardson and His Times,* New York, Museum of Modern Art, 1936.

Huxtable, Ada Louise, *Pier Luigi Nervi,* New York, Braziller, 1960.

Johnson, Philip C., *Mies van der Rohe,* New York, Museum of Modern Art, 1947.

Le Corbusier, *When the Cathedrals Were White,* New York, McGraw-Hill, 1947.

———, *The Modulor,* Cambridge, Harvard, 1948.

———, *Modulor 2 1955,* Cambridge, Harvard, 1958.

———, *Le Corbusier Talks With Students,* New York, Orion, 1961.

McHale, John, *R. Buckminster Fuller,* New York, Braziller, 1962.

Morrison, Hugh, *Louis Sullivan: Prophet of Modern Architecture,* New York, Museum of Modern Art and W. W. Norton, 1935.

Neutra, Richard, *Mystery and Realities of the Site,* Scarsdale, New York, Morgan & Morgan, 1951.

Papadaki, Stamo, *Oscar Niemeyer,* New York, Braziller, 1960.

Scully, Vincent, Jr., *Louis I. Kahn,* New York, Braziller, 1962.

Sullivan, Louis H., *Kindergarten Chats and Other Writings,* New York, Wittenborn, 1947.

Van Rensselaer, Mrs. Schuyler, *Henry Hobson Richardson and His Works,* Boston, Houghton Mifflin, 1888.

Wright, Frank Lloyd, *The Future of Architecture,* New York, Horizon Press, 1953.

Among books that cover the immediate modern field more generally are:

Blake, Peter, *The Master Builders,* New York, Knopf, 1960.

Dalzell, W. R., *Architecture: The Indispensable Art,* London, Michael Joseph, 1962.

Hudnut, Joseph, *Architecture and the Spirit of Man,* Cambridge, Harvard, 1949.

Kultermann, Udo, *Architecture of Today,* New York, Universe Books, 1959.

Lethaby, W. R., *Architecture: An Introduction to the History and Theory of the Art of Building,* New York, Oxford, 1955.

Peter, John, *Masters of Modern Architecture,* New York, Braziller, 1958.

Richards, J. M., *An Introduction to Modern Architecture,* Baltimore, Penguin, 1959.

Scully, Vincent, Jr., *Modern Architecture,* New York, Braziller, 1961.

Zevi, Bruno, *Towards an Organic Architecture,* London, Faber & Faber, 1950.

Some of these writers deserve praise for some special quality. Joseph Hudnut, for instance, is uncommonly readable; Philip C. Johnson is himself an architect as well as a writer. One other man deserves special mention. He is the most prolific and covers the field most thoroughly. His works are essential to every reader:

Mumford, Lewis, *Sticks and Stones: A Study of American Architecture and Civilization,* New York, Boni & Liveright, 1924.

————, *From the Ground Up,* New York, Harvest-Harcourt, Brace & World, 1956.

————, *The City in History,* New York, Harcourt, Brace & World, 1961.

————, *The Highway and the City,* New York, Harvest-Harcourt, Brace & World, 1963.

————, editor, *The Roots of Contemporary American Architecture,* New York, Reinhold, 1952.

A variety of other titles:

Banham, Reyner, *Theory and Design in the First Machine Age,* London, Architectural Press, 1960.

Bannister, Turpin C., editor, *The Architect at Mid-Century: Evolution and Achievement,* New York, Reinhold, 1954.

Behrendt, Walter Curt, *Modern Building,* New York, Harcourt, Brace & World, 1937.

Blake, Peter, *God's Own Junkyard,* New York, Holt, Rinehart & Winston, 1964.

Cheney, Sheldon, *The New World Architecture,* New York, Longmans, Green, 1930.

Giedion, Sigfried, *Space, Time and Architecture,* Cambridge, Harvard, 1943.

Hitchcock, Henry-Russell, *Latin American Architecture Since 1945,* New York, Museum of Modern Art, 1955.

Hughes, Nicholas, Lewison, Grant, and Wesley, Tom, editors, *Cambridge New Architecture,* Cambridge, England, Trinity Hall, 1964.

McLaughlin, Robert W., *Architect,* New York, Macmillan, 1962.

Museum of Modern Art, *Twentieth Century Engineering,* New York, 1964, introduction by Arthur Drexler.

Nekrasov, Viktor, *Both Sides of the Ocean,* New York, Holt, Rinehart & Winston, 1964.

Pevsner, Nikolaus, *An Outline of European Architecture,* New York, Scribner, 1948.

Read, Donald, *The English Provinces c. 1760-1960: A Study in Influence,* London, Arnold, 1964.

Rodman, Selden, *Mexican Journal,* New York, Devin-Adair, 1958.
Rogers, W. G., *When This You See Remember Me: Gertrude Stein in Person,* New York, Rinehart, 1948.
Rogers, W. G., and Weston, Mildred, *Carnival Crossroads: The Story of Times Square,* New York, Doubleday, 1960.
Temko, Allan, *Notre Dame of Paris,* New York, Viking, 1955.
Tunnard, Christopher, and Pushkarev, Boris, *Man-Made America: Chaos or Control?* New Haven, Yale, 1963.
Architectural Forum editors, *Building, U. S. A.,* New York, McGraw-Hill, 1957.

Among the classics there are of course John Ruskin's *The Stones of Venice* and *The Seven Lamps of Architecture,* and Henry Adams' *Mont-Saint-Michel and Chartres.* The student should also read a novel that Frank Lloyd Wright read: Victor Hugo's *Notre Dame de Paris.* The list ends with one essayist and two contemporary novels on the lighter side:

Valéry, Paul, *Dialogues,* New York, Bollingen-Pantheon, 1956.
Gilbert, Edwin, *Native Stone,* New York, Doubleday, 1956.
Hodgins, Eric, *Mr. Blandings Builds His Dream House,* New York, Simon & Schuster, 1946.

Leaflets or pamphlets:

Noguchi, Isamu, *Explanation of the Sculpture Garden of the Beinecke Rare Book and Manuscript Library, Yale University,* released by library, 1964.
Iglesia de la Medalla Milagrosa, Mexico, D. F.
The Cathedral Church of St. Michael, Coventry, Stockport, England, Cloister Press, 1962.

Index

186